M000202231

DREAM BOLDLY, I DARE YOU II

Course II: Manifest Miracles OnDemand

Inspiration from today's thought leaders, best-selling authors, motivational speakers and world-class coaches

Compiled by Carrie Stepp

Printed in the United States of America
First Printing: 2017
ISBN: 0996779159
ISBN-13: 978-0996779159

Stepp Enterprises Inc. | 47724 SD Hwy 50 | Elk Point, SD 57025
Website: CarrieStepp.com | Carrie@eLearningSuccessCoach.com
All rights reserved.

This book is for

_____

With love from

_____

SPECIAL ACKNOWLEDGEMENTS

I'd like to send a special thank you to the beautiful leaders, teachers, healers and world changers, who have made this divinely guided project possible. They have entrusted me with their most sacred testimonies by opening their hearts and souls, to heal and empower our world in which we all share. Prepare to step into the sovereign being you came here to be, and dare to dream boldly.

TABLE OF CONTENTS

INSPIRING LIFE PURPOSE, PASSION & MISSION

ENLIGHTENING LOVE, FAMILY & RELATIONSHIPS

EMPOWERING HEALING MIND, BODY & SPIRIT

INTRODUCTION

The power to command miracles resides within us.
You are being invited to free your possibilities;
to embody your highest potential; to remember
what you came here for. You are an infinite being
of light. It's time to step into the sovereign being
you came here to be.

This extraordinary book of transformation contains
31 days of inspiring and healing life testimonies,
intended to be savored one by one. Begin each
morning or close each day with a profound
message that's certain to awaken pure potential.
Today is a gift. Remember to unwrap it fully.

Join our unbreakable chain of love, as you embark
on this transformational journey to dream boldly.
Each book contains a key to unlock an eLearning
course to Manifest Miracles OnDemand.

DREAM BOLDLY, I DOUBLE DARE YOU!

WITH LOVE, CARRIE STEPP

From the depths of my heart, I thank you and honor you for linking onto our chain of friendship that you're about to experience. This is the second book in our Dream Boldly series. Our first book takes you on a journey to begin unlocking the deepest desires of your heart, and shares our Dream Boldly Challenge: 100 Dreams in 10 Days. You're welcome to visit DreamBoldly.org to download our free templates.

Within this book that you've just been gifted, we're expanding upon the first, so we'll be taking you further, deeper and wider. Thank you for joining us on this adventure to unveil truth, shed the lies, and release fears, so that you may spread your wings and fly along with us; as we continue to heal, inspire and empower deeply.

As we begin, I'd like to connect each of you who have chosen to take this journey along with us, as it's no accident that you're here with us right now.

My family and I live in rural South Dakota, with a creek that flows along our acreage. An abundance of trees grow all along the water's edge. Each tree stands individually; though the supply received, all comes from the same source.

Imagine for a moment that it has just started raining and as the drops are collected, the stream is beginning to flow. The flow of water begins to rise. As the roots of a tree do, the water begins filling you up through your feet. You feel it moving up into your body until you feel fully nourished. The body of water continues to flow through you and into each of our writers as you connect with each of their stories. As the creek curves around the bend, the water continues...

CARRIE STEPP

Carrie Stepp is the Creator of Dream Boldly. As a global thought leader specializing in transformative personal and professional development, she's on a bold mission to inspire, heal and empower our world. She's a Midwestern country girl full of heart & branded in technology. Master Teacher is her life's purpose. She's invested 23 years as an Award-Winning Master Course Designer, Inventor, International Best-Selling Author and Intuitive Creator who guides leaders in bringing dreams to life in living color. Learn more at CarrieStepp.com or email Carrie@eLearningSuccessCoach.com.

FREE YOUR POSSIBILITIES

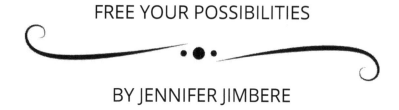

BY JENNIFER JIMBERE

I cannot begin to share with you, the sheer gratitude I feel for helping others realize that what they think is possible, is just the beginning. I help leaders globally free their possibilities, and I'd love to tell you about one of them, to invite you to dream boldly as well.

She was working so hard that she was missing out on life. She was spinning her wheels daily and stuck in the whirlwind of her business. As a mother of three, and wife of twenty-six years, she was lost, frustrated and feeling overwhelmed. She knew something had to change.

I received her call about a year ago, when she shared, "I am not sure how you can help me, but I know I cannot keep trying to do this alone, and somehow I just know that you can support me."

As a coach, when I talk to people, I'm curious about their current reality and their goals. When we got on our first coaching call together, she shared with me some of her priorities, as well as her perception of how things were coming along in her life. At first, she talked a lot about how she was

12

progressing professionally. She shared that when she was promoted, her family, friends, and co-workers, would wonder and ask why she needed to move onto the next role, when she had a great career already? She was questioning herself and kept thinking, "shouldn't I just be happy with what I've already achieved?"

You see, sometimes we can be cruising through our lives on a hedonic treadmill and not even recognize it! We can be focused on the wrong things, while attempting to bring more happiness into our lives. The hedonic treadmill, also known as hedonic adaptation, is the observed tendency of humans to quickly return to a relatively stable level of happiness, despite major positive or negative events or life changes.

I invited her to slow down and listen to the critical and sometimes negative thoughts of others, as well as her own as it came to her professional life, and write them down over the course of two weeks. When we reviewed them together, she began to realize that she recognized the thoughts she payed attention to, had been programmed since childhood. One of her top character strengths is the love of learning, and through this reflection, she came to realize that life can also be a series of unlearning what's been wired into us, as much as it is about learning new things.

Imagine for a moment, that even though we might be

thirty, forty or fifty, it's possible to still be running the programming from when we were five years old. Our beliefs such as "money doesn't grow on trees" or "you should be thankful you have a job," are words that can keep us locked into that pattern until the day we die.

Once we begin to break out of those thoughts, we wonder how we didn't learn to question these thought patterns earlier? The school system is designed to help us gather information. The books pile up and we get tested. We call this learning.

Please don't get me wrong; I have over thirteen degrees and certifications, so I believe education is a key that opens possibilities. However, this is not learning. This is gathering information and storing it. There is a difference between learning and gathering information. School taught us valuable information, but it never taught us how to alter our old paradigms, how to manage self-doubt, and when it creeps up, we may not have the strategies to overcome it. Sometimes, a happier, healthier life means undoing some of the well-meaning advice we were given.

We were able to identify which areas of my client's life she really wanted to improve the most, using the Circle of Personal Perspective tool. When I took her through the exercise, she was shocked at which area she most wanted to have increased satisfaction in. It wasn't her professional life at all! She was given the time and space to really think, to pause and focus on herself, and was asked great questions. She realized what was most important, and wanted to create an action plan to increase the level of satisfaction in that area of her life.

When I studied traditional psychology, I realized the focus was on bringing someone to a line, to operate at a functional level in society. When I began to learn and study positive psychology, or the science of well-being, I learned that there is a focus on bringing people above the line, into thriving. I've studied in this field for hundreds of hours and have learned countless practices based on research.

Together, my client and I worked on what was most important for her. She was open to trying a new morning routine, she said new mantra's, she shifted her perspective, and took inspired actions daily to improve that area of her life. In turn, other areas improved as well!

When we began working together, she rated that area on the circle of personal perspective as a 4, on a scale of 1-10. The scale on this tool goes from 1 (being not at all satisfied) to 10 (being absolutely thrilled) with that area of life.

Today, we still work together from time to time to continue to improve the additional areas of her personal and professional life that she'd like to maximize. She now rates that area of her life as an 8! Some major improvements have happened in her life over the past year. She is feeling more in control and fully supported, because she is open and receptive to additional help, and she is living with more ease and enjoyment. She now knows she has the power to free new possibilities in her life!

To manifest something, it needs to be clear or obvious to the eye or mind. She needed a partner in possibility to help her believe that what she wanted was available to her, and that she could bring it into being. We're always manifesting. Each thought we have creates an energy flow within and around our physical beings. This energy attracts its likeness. So, if you're thinking, "I suck," then your energy kind of, well, sucks. You are creative, capable, wise and good, and "suck" is not what we want to attract!

The opposite experience also occurs when we think thoughts like, "I rock!" When we think, feel, and believe a thought like "I rock," we exude an energy of confidence, and in turn attract great experiences into our life. Each thought we have informs our energy, and our energy manifests into our experiences. Our thoughts and energy create our reality. I believe we can choose to make it a great day; and if we do that daily, we can create a great life for ourselves.

If we truly want to use our energetic power to manifest

greatness, we must clear all that blocks us from believing in our greatness. When we partner with someone to help clear the blocks, we begin to clean them up to clear space for positive manifestations to occur.

Below are 3 key principles for genuine manifesting. When practicing these steps, make sure to stay committed to the goal of feeling good first, and attracting stuff second. Continue to remind yourself that when you feel good, you energetically attract goodness into your life. When our primary function is to be happy, then whatever comes up is irrelevant. Happiness is our true manifestation!

KEY PRINCIPLES FOR MANIFESTING

1. Allow time to pause.
2. Get clear.
3. Feel it, see it, believe it.

I'd also like to share a mantra that I invite you to try, to free new possibilities into your life, "I am open and receptive to all good!" Clients that have used this daily begin to see shifts in their lives. Grant yourself permission to be on the lookout for good things. Once we train our brains to see the good, we do!

Discover what works best for you, and make a conscious effort to change, or "unlearn" that which doesn't serve you. In the unlearning process, I invite you to move away from what you've been taught, and move towards what your spirit says.

Do you feel stuck in an area of your life that you know you can improve upon? This is your invitation to soar, and go after that luscious life of your dreams! What do you need to unlearn to make that happen, and free your possibilities?

Begin with three key questions to free your possibilities:

1. When was the last time I allowed myself to dream?
2. How can I share all the knowledge I have acquired?
3. What is the legacy I wish to leave behind?

What you think is possible is just the beginning!

JENNIFER JIMBERE

Jennifer Jimbere is the President of Jimbere Coaching and Consulting, and Co-Founder & resident Thrive Expert of The Radical Joy Seeking Women's Club. She is also the Co-Founder of OM Akademy. She shares proven, action oriented, research based applications in the areas of coaching, change Management and the science of well-being. Jennifer is a published author in the book Dream Boldly, I Dare You. Learn more by visiting www.jimberecoachingandconsulting.com and www.radicaljoyseekingwomen.com. Twitter: jenniferjimbere Facebook: www.facebook.com/jimberecoachingandconsulting

UNVEILED

BY CARRIE ROARK

My hand hovered over the double light switch to extinguish the fluorescents that had illuminated my days for the past four years. It struck me that I was about to walk out of this room for the last time. I didn't want to miss the significance of this moment, so I stopped and turned around. I glanced back at the classroom that had been my home, as the Jr. High English teacher for a private school. The bulletin boards were bare. My posters were tucked away in my poster protector. My personal items lay in the box at my feet. My eyes stopped at the front of the room, the space I claimed five times each day as I welcomed my sweet students.

Memories flashed before my mind's eye. From that space at the front of the room, I had taught, challenged, inspired, and entertained. I reminisced over the inside jokes and felt the laughter in my belly. I remembered the times I strayed from my lesson plans, to follow my instincts that told me my students needed to hear something else at certain moments. My heart filled with love and I prayed blessings over the students who would sit in the chairs next year, with someone else teaching in my spot.

It was a brief moment, but it was also a full moment. I was grateful for it all. With a slight nod, I turned to walk out one last time. My hand dropped down over the switches, and the room fell into darkness. It was a great four years. I loved it, and I was good at it. And yet, I left with anticipation and joy at what was to come next.

You see, I had resigned my position as the teacher, to finally follow my dreams. I had chosen to leave something I was good at, to chase something that I am great at. As I write today, it is the first day of summer. While other teachers are gearing down for their much-deserved rest, I'm gearing up to begin a new and exciting chapter.

So, how did I get here? This is the story I want to share. It's the story you need to hear if you've been hiding from something, if you've been waiting for something, or blinded by something. I hope my story will inspire you to chase your dreams too. You see, you aren't living up to your potential, and that's starting to get on my nerves. You were fearfully and wonderfully made to accomplish great things, and to live a life of abundance. To do anything less is an insult to your creator.

Two years ago, I began to adopt new philosophies that slowly changed my life. A friend introduced me to the book "Do Hard Things" by Alex Harris. It points out that as humans, we tend to avoid anything hard. The problem with this, is that it is only when we are challenged, that we can grow. John Maxwell says that "everything worthwhile in life is uphill." In this case, I had better start climbing.

Bradley, my husband, and I were introduced to personal growth and development tools, and we quickly gained a voracious appetite. Like saplings, we began to grow and change. This was how I was introduced to another philosophy that changed my life. What we focus on expands, or what we think about, we bring about. This is the Law of Attraction. I learned how our thoughts have incredible power to influence our experiences in life. It became clear to me that negative cycles remained in my life, because my thoughts remained negative. Scarcity and debt latched onto me because subconsciously, I allowed it to. The more anxious and worried I felt, I'd only draw more worry and anxiety to myself. I held a mindset that money and blessings were scarce and only for certain people. It was a belief I picked up as a child. Mom would say, "People in hell want ice water." In an effort to protect me from disappointment, she ended up teaching me that it wasn't ok to want more in life. People don't really get what they want, so it's best not to want anything. This is a mindset born out of fear and it carries the name "scarcity mindset." When you expect things to be scarce, they will be for you.

This was a huge revelation for me. My eyes were opened to the fact that I had been held hostage by fear. This fear-based mindset kept me from choosing actions that would propel me into a new direction, a direction toward abundance. Here is a simple example of how mindset makes a difference. I had once returned a paper to one of my 8th grade students that was filled with spelling mistakes. When he got the paper back, he said in his typical self-deprecating humor, "I can't spell." I stopped him and said, "Let's reframe that. What if instead of telling yourself that I can't spell, you say, I can't spell that word yet?" He thought about it for a minute.

I said, "What would you do, if you believed you couldn't spell a word?" He replied without missing a beat, "Nothing. I'd just guess at it and go on." I continued, "Well, what would you do if you said to yourself, I can't spell that word yet?" He said, "I'd look it up and learn it." "Yes! That's right." This is a perfect example of how mindset can propel you nowhere or somewhere.

How you set your mind makes all the difference in your life. I began to practice mindset principles by getting up a bit earlier each morning and repeating positive affirmations such as, "Wealth is abundant, and I can have what I go after." Another was "I can do all things through Christ who gives me strength." This one is a bible scripture found in Philippians 4:13. Bible

23

verses make fantastic affirmations! Another affirmation I hold closely is "It's an amazing day! I feel amazing, God is amazing, I'm amazing, and something amazing is going to happen today."

This practice began to awaken old longings from within me. I enjoy writing, but didn't write much because I was afraid. I would tell myself that I was busy, or tired, or whatever excuse was handy. Looking back, I can see fear is what held me back. I have a driving desire to be admired in all things. This comes from an insecurity to seek validation and approval from others, so I feared anything that ran the risk of me looking foolish or stupid. Besides, writing is hard, and I worked hard at avoiding hard things!

Years ago, I attempted to find my purpose and the question was asked "What gives you the most joy?" In the movie Chariots of Fire, Eric Lidell says, "When I run, I feel His pleasure." We were asked to consider the times when we most felt God's pleasure. Writing immediately came to mind. This was fifteen years ago, so why wasn't I writing? I remembered Mom's words about the people in hell, and what they received when they wanted things. Writing was for someone else, as I didn't have whatever I thought a writer needed. I'd write a bit here and there, but never with any seriousness.

What I wanted more than anything, was to follow in Beth Moore's footsteps, to write and teach Bible studies. Really. I longed to be Beth Moore. Oh, I hope she reads this one day. Beth, you are my idol and my role model! Well, I have the southern accent, but that is where the comparison ends. I am not Beth Moore, and I never will be. I am Carrie Roark. I'm not a great writer. I have no experience teaching. Yes, I see the irony of that statement coming from a school teacher. This is what I'm trying to tell you. My mind was full of lies! Fear is deceptive and devious. Now, back to my list; I'm not attractive, I'm fat, and I have a terrible wardrobe. I felt the desire to be a public speaker, but fears arose. I'd spoken a few times for church groups and enjoyed the electricity rushing through me, but my husband Bradley took more naturally to speaking in front of others.

Surprisingly, my mentor in our MLM business asked me to conduct a presentation. I freaked out, but accepted the challenge. I prepared what to say, I crafted the words, memorized, and practiced immensely. So, how did it go? I killed it! Afterwards, several told me it was the best presentation they'd seen. With this, Bradley and I began to dream of working together as authors, speakers, and coaches and became certified by John Maxwell's team.

We weren't sure we could make it all happen. I wanted to resign, to pursue this passion, but we'd be losing the steady paycheck and it was scary. I feared we would do something we'd regret. Then, during a bible study, our teacher shared two spiritual veils from 2 Corinthians 3. One veil keeps us from clearly seeing the things of God. The other veil is held when we hide our faith, instead of declaring our faith to the world. As I listened, I wrote the question "Do I have any lingering veils in my life? Are there veils preventing me from seeing clearly or veils I hide behind?"

As the questions marinated, thoughts came to mind. I didn't want people to know about my dreams, because they may judge me. I also didn't need to stop working to write and teach. I could do both in my spare time! Following our bible study that night, I declared to the ladies that I am a bible teacher and that I was coming out from behind my veil to claim that. I felt unveiled and empowered!

During our next bible study, God spoke to me again. As I listened to the teaching, everything clicked into place. Our teacher shared that we are each apportioned a unique assignment. I wrote "There is space for me. I don't need someone else's assignment." She encouraged us to seek only the commendation of God. A quote that stood out to me was "When the Lord entrusts you with a ministry assignment, you will not only delight in it, you'll be able to rest in it." Now that my unique assignment was clear, it felt wrong not to accept it. I can't explain it really, but a knowing pervaded my heart that I was ready to resign at the end of the school year. I no longer waffled.

I just knew it was what I wanted.

I couldn't wait to get home that night to tell Bradley what had happened in my heart. Fear, anxiety, and worry had simply vanished. Bradley was delighted with my decision, and a few days later I turned in my letter of resignation. That next week we signed a corporate training contract equating to more income than my annual salary. I couldn't help but recite my newest affirmation, "Money is plentiful and flows freely to us every day. God, I thank you for your bounty." We soon received two more contracts and we haven't really even started yet. As soon as we stepped into faith, to follow our unique assignment, our prayers were answered. Thank you, God, for your abundance and bounty!

What about you? What sends electricity up and down your spine? When do you feel God's pleasure, and what gives you the most joy? John Maxwell says, "Life is like a ten-speed bike. Most of us have gears we never use." If you aren't operating at your capacity, know that you can. Maybe you need to grow first. This is where coaching can help. Find a coach that resonates, read and listen to motivational speakers. Research mindset and start practicing those strategies today. God told me during our bible study, "There is room for you and your dreams. You too have been apportioned a unique assignment.

Will you go get it?"

27

Today, we're not only following our dreams, we're chasing them! We continue to grow and saturate our minds with further teachings. I'm overjoyed to see what God has in store. Watch out world, here I come, and I'm bringing friends! Dare to dream boldly!

CARRIE ROARK

Carrie Roark is on a mission! She lived forty years stuck in negative cycles, until she learned about the power of our mindset. As an author and a certified coach with the John Maxwell Team, she'll teach you how to think about how you think. Her services are for those who long for more, but are unsure how to find it. Jumpstart results fast with a VIP day session designed to bring results quickly. Mention Dream Boldly to receive a free Power Hour. Purchase her "My Daily Focus Planning Journal" from Amazon or visit her website to live a life of intention and keep your goals front and center. Visit www.roarkcc.com.

WE ARE NECESSARY, NOT OPTIONAL

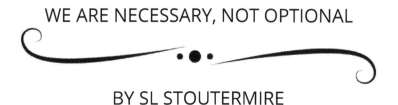

BY SL STOUTERMIRE

One of the most difficult questions we are forced to consider in life is, "What am I supposed to be doing?" "What is my purpose?" "Why do I feel so restless in everything I'm doing?" I've had to ask myself these questions many times, and when I finally discovered the answer, I never looked back.

Many of us have struggled with these questions, but we refuse to go deeper in the thought process to find the answers we need. It's a very daunting task, to truly search within ourselves and find those missing pieces of us. For me, it was also difficult to let go of those pieces that weren't meant to be a part of me.

Years ago, I began my career working at a bank. After some time, I started my own business, but not necessarily the way it should have been conceived. When I was first given the vision of owning a business, it was to serve people. As I began my business, I started to allow the draw of money to be my guide. I accepted the clients who could afford to pay me the most money, to be their business consultant, to write their business plans and grants, turn their companies around financially, write and develop new programs for them, etc. I specialized in helping others in so many expansive ways, that I began to question my sole purpose. I truly knew that God had blessed me with a number of gifts and talents to help those who couldn't typically afford these services, yet here I was so far from where I was supposed to be.

I didn't realize it, but I had become their employee, instead of my own employer. Now before I go any further, let me explain my statement. As an entrepreneur, we are always someone's employee. However, I was the employee (not because I was hired by the person, organization or company) but because I was enslaved to the income that was derived from only taking on certain clients. I wasn't serving in the depth I was supposed to be.

I was constantly frustrated, because my entire reason for going into business was to make a difference. I didn't see a difference being made. I became cynical. It started to affect my outlook on so many things and people (including myself). The moment I realized this, I knew I had to make some changes, with a great deal of struggle, prayer, and finally acceptance.

First, I had to start by asking myself some very serious questions, that only I could truly answer for me. Here are some of the questions that I asked. "What is it that I love doing more than anything else? Do I enjoy the current career field I'm in, but not the current position? Do I feel as if I should be helping someone else, such as the sick? What am I being called here to do?" As I explored these questions, I spent time praying and seeking true guidance from the Holy Spirit. I pondered these questions and listened for the right answers. Once I knew I wasn't where I was supposed to be in my career, I gave myself permission to walk through the process of accepting my true purpose and begin shifting towards it.

Sometimes, we may be required to take baby steps toward our vision, and other times we may have to take the leap of faith and go for it. No matter what, don't allow fear and a lack of faith to hinder you. As I started the transition, I constantly had to remind myself that while it may seem difficult in the beginning, I would eventually arrive at the point of the greatest breakthroughs I've ever experienced in my life! I believed these breakthroughs would bring me more joy and peace than I had ever experienced, and it would be immeasurable. Isn't that the goal, to fulfill our purpose and be at peace? All I truly wanted, was to be who I was truly meant to be in this life. I knew that I wouldn't be able to measure my success at the beginning of the process. For some, success can't be measured at all! We are all called to be or do something with our own personal gifts and talents. That nagging feeling of being incomplete, was like an annoying alarm clock telling me it was time to get back into my own lane. If we get into a lane that's not meant for us, we'll begin feeling frustrated, rushed, tired, unhappy, and going nowhere fast.

To prevent myself from continually experiencing these negative feelings, I had to be willing to take the risk and move towards my passion and mission in life. I had to dream boldly about my plans and refuse to allow the thoughts of others to change my mind or create self-doubt. There will always be critics and detractors. Everyone will not, and cannot, understand your purpose, choices and vision. Some of these may even be your closest friends and family. Please accept that the vision wasn't meant for them, and move on. Yes, it hurts, especially when it's people close to you, but you cannot allow that negativity to stop you from being your true self. You can choose to tune them out as you continue pressing forward.

Next, I had to be willing to believe in myself. If I couldn't believe in me, then how could I expect anyone else to believe in me? I realized that I could only fail, if I never tried. I was strong enough to continue, and I know you are too, so we must be willing to put in the work. Things didn't come together all at once. It took time, patience and dedication. I refused to give up. I kept trying. I failed forward. The greater the goal, the greater our determination and focus will need to be, to reach our goals. This doesn't come easy and no one else can do our work for us.

33

They won't know our passion, nor vision for the work we're intended to do. I'll be honest, that I often burn the midnight oil and skip sleep during the day, but I always listen when I know I'm being called, and finish the assignment that's been set before me.

There will be times we get frustrated or want to throw in the towel. It's during these times, when I remind myself of how unhappy I was, at a job I didn't even like doing. I remind myself that I had been spending my time working and fulfilling someone else's mission, while feeling depleted every day. I tell myself it's time to get back to work, and stop allowing myself to be distracted. I was a bank account that only had withdrawals coming out, but no deposits coming in. I knew I would eventually be overdrawn. As I complete each mission, I sit back and reflect on how great I feel pursuing my own passions. I assess how great it is to accomplish my own goals. While there's deep work involved, pursuing our passions brings peace. I am useful. I am joyous. I am healed. I am whole. I am home.

Today, I serve not only those who can afford it, but I serve further, deeper and wider. My services are centered around helping others rediscover themselves and find their purpose. As my mission expands, my services and reach expand too. As long as I'm here, I'll continue to expand and grow. I'm no longer using my gifts and talents; they now use me, and I love it! I encourage you to find your purpose. The longer you wait, the further you are from arriving. Don't wait to reflect back upon your life and be filled with a lot of "what ifs" and thoughts of what could have been. The only person or thing stopping you from starting that business, writing that book, or serving in that capacity, is you!

I double dare you to dream boldly enough, and to reach deep inside yourself to find what's inside of you waiting to be fulfilled. Our world needs your passion, your vision, your niche, all of you! We are necessary, not optional!

SL STOUTERMIRE

SL Stoutermire lives in Alabama with her husband and seven wonderful kids. They enjoy spending time together as a family and serving God in the capacities they've been called to serve. She's committed to sharing her testimony, so that no one ever feels alone in their experiences. She's the Author of several books, a business consultant and motivational speaker who serves passionately. Learn more at www.slstoutermire.com.

THE JOURNEY BACK TO MY TRUE SELF

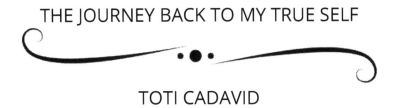

TOTI CADAVID

I used to be a hard-core and very driven business woman, but I am not that person anymore. This is a story of true survival, of being lost and being found. It is a story of life lessons, of understanding what is truly important in our lives. It is a story of transformation; of finally being inspired to do what is right for humanity, and truly following my heart.

There was a time when what used to make me proud of myself was reaching every goal I ever put in front of me, no matter how difficult it was or who stood in my way to achieve it. To me, confusion and failure were states of mind I thought were only for weaker individuals. Although none of that is technically "wrong," what made it all wrong was that I wasn't following my heart. My life was set and driven by others, and I was the puppet performing to their every desire. As time went on, I got more and more disconnected from my real self, and from what my heart desired deep down. So, the Universe, as smart as it is, had to intervene, but let's just say that since I was too busy to pay attention to the subtler ways in which it was trying to wake me up; more drastic measures were taken, to bring me down from the cloud I was living in. I was forced to understand what and who was truly important, and it took literally tearing my life into pieces and crushing everything I believed in; to be *real*, for me to finally get a clue.

It was totally dark. I couldn't understand where we were, or why our minivan wasn't moving. The last thing I remembered was that we were on our way back to the condo where our children were peacefully sleeping. "What happened?" "We crashed," said my husband in a cracked voice. I'm not sure if I had woken up from being unconscious or fell asleep after that crash, but what I do know is that nothing was ever the same after I woke up. I tried to look around, but could only see some dim lights far away. I tried to open the door, but couldn't. I started crawling to the back of the van, but when I tried to push myself with my foot, I felt an excruciating pain in my right foot. I knew something was wrong with it.

As painful as it was to walk away from that accident with a fractured neck, a broken foot, and many bruises, the physical pain was nothing compared to the inner pain and sadness of my heart. I was totally broken. Those first days after the accident are a blur in my mind. On the outside, we followed medical instructions, welcomed the loving advice from family members, and eventually made it back to our home in Colorado. But, something inside me had changed. I tried to get back to my usual routine, but I couldn't. I think that my mind was trying to make sense of something only my soul could understand. Nothing in my life seemed to make sense anymore. It was as if the person who I was before had died in the accident, and just my body had come back to Colorado. I was completely lost.

I didn't understand it then, but the Universe had been trying to wake me up, and I kept on refusing to stop long enough to pay attention and analyze my actions. I was too selfish and ego-driven to realize a change of course was necessary. This accident moved everything within and outside of me. My thoughts kept focusing on the fact that this was the second time I had faced death. My first encounter had taken place four years earlier when I found myself septic and dying from an infection in my blood. The situation was so critical that a priest came in to read my last rites. After he left, I begged God to give me another chance to live, because my three children were too little. I promised to put my life and my priorities in order. It was time for a soul realignment. It worked! Things took a turn for the better overnight, and I was able to leave the intensive care unit a week later.

I meant to keep my promise to God, but it only lasted a few months, until I felt well enough to get back to my routine of working with clients, events, networking, business development, etc. My firm was doing really well and it demanded a lot from me. Years went on, and nothing changed until that rainy night when we crashed into that side of a mountain and miraculously survived.

Upon reflection after the accident, I started to feel so guilty about my broken promises to God. I had promised to stop working so hard, to allow myself to become a better mother, to put my priorities in place, but I wasn't fulfilling my promises. Why didn't I? Was God now punishing me with this accident for not having done everything I said I would do?

I kept questioning everything about myself, the poor decisions I made that brought me to this broken state, and the deplorable state of my "BEingness." At some point in my life, I had gone from being a hard-working 24-year-old single mother who was doing everything she could to make something good out of her life, tirelessly working full time while going to school at night to complete a bachelor's and two master's degrees, while lovingly caring for her special needs child, to an egotistical individual who just cared about achieving more of everything. When did I become that individual who was so focused on reaching more financial success, accumulating more material possessions, and being recognized as a successful leader? When did I start making excuses for not caring enough about the people I was hurting with my behavior? I had increasingly been paying less and less attention to everything and everyone that really mattered. I had focused on what I thought was success, and had let everything else in my life fall apart.

My reality sucked, but it sucked even more because I knew that at one point in my life, I felt like I did have it all. There was no goal placed in front of me that I had not achieved. I declared great success in my career and I reached it. I had great careers that had allowed me to travel the world and climb the ladder in corporate America. I became a very successful entrepreneur and took my company to seven figures. I was recognized and awarded for the work I did in the community a great number of times. After realizing my first marriage should have never happened, I fell in love with a great guy, only to take him for granted. I adored my special needs son with all my heart, but also wanted to be a mom of children that didn't have so many health challenges. God blessed me with two more healthy children. I had great friends, and had always been able to buy and do anything I ever wanted.

I wasn't always ego-driven, but somewhere on my journey to success, my life took the wrong turn and I became entitled. I failed to appreciate my blessings, and started seeing everything that was wrong in my world. I complained to God and fought with him for punishing my adored son with more and more serious health problems that required major surgeries. I kept focusing on every fault my husband had and kept trying to change him. I sadly found plenty of wrongs in friends, family and co-workers. Unfortunately, the more wrongs I found in people, and in my life, the more challenges and negative things I was confronted with. Meanwhile, I believed I was so perfect, so right, so gifted, that I became this arrogant, full-of-myself individual who believed most everyone else wasn't up to par with me. I was too busy and my time was too valuable to take the time it required to keep extended family and friends close by. I became an absent mom, with the excuse of a very demanding work load and schedule. I basically became the worse possible version of me, yet I couldn't see it, nor admit it. I was too perfect and everyone else who complained about it was just wrong.

The first year after the accident was emotionally chaotic. That accident woke me up to see my true reality. I was faced daily with the terrible guilt and pain of seeing the consequences of my wrong decisions. I was finally able to see and admit my wrongs, but had no idea how to mend so much wrong. Could my marriage and my relationships with my kids be mended? Would those friends I had become too busy and too important for, give me another chance? Could my extended family love me again? I was so down, that it began affecting my ability and desire to work. I began to care less and less, as it seemed pointless to do my job when everything else in my life wasn't working. I didn't know where to start and my guilt and embarrassment kept me from even trying. I fell into a deep depression, and wanted out of life. Worse, instead of admitting my own wrongs, I became more arrogant and demanding at work. I started to lose clients, my then business partner did a number on me, and I began to lose more clients and employees. As my firm crumbled, my life quickly flew downhill. There was nothing working for me. The whole world seemed to be up against me. Living from the glass half-empty perspective completely depleted me. My depression got the best of me, life didn't seem to be worth living, and I collapsed.

The only good thing that happened throughout all this time is that somehow, somewhere inside of me, a desire to heal was still present. How that was still there, I do not know. Maybe there's a sense of humanity inside all of us, but the road to healing was not clear. I didn't know where to even begin this healing and transformation process. I started to see a psychiatrist and went to weekly therapy for two years, but nothing changed. I kept going into a deeper hole, while desperately clinging to a dim ray of hope. After two years of weekly therapy sessions, I realized it wasn't taking me to a better place, so I quit. Yes, I quit!

I decided to take a different route and began to work with a coach. I started to realize where and why my life got derailed. This discovery process was as if someone was taking the curtains off my eyes and allowing me to see clearly. The excitement of finding some hope got me more determined to change how I was experiencing my life. It was really hard work, physically and emotionally draining, but within a few months, I was finally able to see that there was still some light. My coach helped me see things from a different perspective, understand what and who was important to me, and guided me on how I could build a life worth living.

I now understood why I had thought that life was about being successful, having more, accumulating more and being recognized for it. I sadly realized that I had tirelessly worked on reaching ego-driven goals and desires, that only created empty success. The type of success that still makes us empty even as we're reaching goals. I had been running my career with my head, and not my heart. Wanting to have more financial abundance was not the issue. The problem lied in not knowing why I wanted it, in believing in society's idea of success instead of defining my own, and in having allowed my ego to become addicted to success and to everything that came with it.

Here is where my new chapter began, once I understood that my life derailed when I lost my purpose. I lost my way, when I failed to have a "heart reason" for working so hard. It doesn't matter where we start; it only matters how we finish.

Within that heavy storm, I knew I had to keep moving

forward for my three children who still valued me, even when I wasn't being a good mom. Nick, my special needs son, needed a loving mom to help him go through all his health troubles, and my two little ones who were then six- and seven-year-olds, still needed a loving and guiding mom in their lives. Armed with my love for them as my driver for change, I began to figure out what type of mom I wanted to be. I started with the end in mind, by asking myself the following question "if I were a ninety-year-old woman looking back at my life, what type of mother, wife, daughter, sister, friend and human being would make me proud?" I then decided to become exactly that type of human being that my heart wanted me to be, and who my loved ones deserved.

I left the daily burden and became a fervent student of any program and every book that promised to deliver insights into finding myself and my true life's purpose. It wasn't easy, because it required that I find my *real* self again who was buried deep down many layers of beliefs that were no longer serving. Change was hard. Removing outdated beliefs was very hard. Acquiring the humbleness required to recognize my faults, mistakes, and demons was extremely hard. However, my three amazing children were my daily inspiration. I declared that if I achieved nothing else in life, I will become the loving, caring and wise mother they deserved! I added other goals as I began to see progress, because I wanted to also become the wife, sister, daughter, friend and leader of my dreams. The enlightenment through this process was not learning how to change my behavior, it was about changing the state of my mind. It is only when we change our mindset, that we can see who we want to be and what we want to change.

It was extremely rewarding to see that as I began to change, my children responded beautifully to having the *real* me back in their life. My relationship with my husband began to feel possible again, friends and extended family came back into my life and I into theirs. It was miraculous! I had found my purpose. I was so inspired by the miracles in my life, that I wanted to guide people in going through the same process to wake up and build the lives and businesses they dream about.

With renewed hope and being full of life, I enrolled in coaching school and opened U-Fulfilled, a leadership and executive coaching company. Imagine that; a company with a real purpose beyond being profitable, with me at the helm! Soon after, I got my first client, then the second, and it continues. As I evolve, my business is evolving too, and is presently transforming into Essencialize, which is the coming home of one's essence. I now see my life through such a different lens and feel very blessed to be able to do such purposeful work for a living. Financial success is great because it allows us to have more fun in life, but it is not the reason I work. Helping others build the lives of their dreams is my purpose, and the driver that keeps me fueled. I feel blessed to do the most fulfilling life-work that I do, as it continues to inspire me to keep my priorities in place.

My children are my most precious gifts, and have been the most wonderful gifts God ever gave to me. They've been the most amazing teachers in my life. I treasure them more than words can explain. I feel very blessed to also have a loving relationship with my husband, to be surrounded by the love of my extended family, and for the amazing friends I get to walk with on this journey we call life with. My only regret that I have, is not going through this transformation sooner.

To all the beautiful souls out there longing to change any aspect of your lives, I tell you that transformation is not only possible, but it will be one of the most rewarding experiences you've ever witnessed. I invite you to pause and get clear about what you want to create with your life, who you want to be, and the experiences you want to create for the people you care so much about. I urge you to passionately go after becoming your true self and creating the life of your dreams. As one of the wisest self-development gurus of the last century said, "Change the way you look at things, and the things you look at will change." - Dr. Wayne Dyer

TOTI CADAVID

Toti Cadavid is a seasoned multicultural branding, marketing and communications strategist with expertise in domestic and international markets. After a second near death experience, Toti went through a transformational journey to find purpose, meaning and inner alignment. She's a bestselling author, speaker, trainer, certified coach, and has launched a branding and leadership development company that helps business leaders build real personal leadership and success. Toti holds a degrees in International Business, Marketing & Organizational Development, and is certified in Entrepreneurship. Connect @ www.Ufulfilled.com or www.Essencialize.com.

DARING TO BE YOU

BY DORTE ERTBOLL

My bags were ready, stacks of books to read and carefully planned holiday clothes I longed to wear. We always spent a month in the same place under the hot southern French sun and it was a major annual highlight. But this time our plans were abruptly changed, and this quickly became the biggest turmoil I'd experienced.

At twelve years old, I honestly hadn't seen much turmoil up to that point. Even if I had, nothing could have prepared me for what was to come next. That's the way it is with major life events. They invade you, flood you like a giant tsunami, and take over your reality and perception of what's normal and safe, forcing you to somehow make sense of this new reality while feeling that you're hanging on by a thread.

We lost her. My mum. In the space of a few months she was gone, and nothing was ever the same again for any of us. How could anything ever be the same when you lose one of the most central and loved people in your life? Nothing can ever go back to the way it was, because it is no more. It's gone.

Thirty-something years later, I discovered my marriage

was over. The same feeling of overwhelm invaded me at first. How could he not be happy? How could we not be happy? We had come so far. We had created so much together! Our story was so entangled, that a life apart did not even feel like an option. But just like my mum, that life too was gone, and I felt lost. There was too much hurt, pain and disappointment to be able to see the future clearly.

Everything changed color. Nothing tasted the same. Everything needed a new meaning. I had no idea how to go on from there. I had no idea how I would even start. I was paralyzed in confusion, fear, sadness and pain. It was huge, enormous, scary, impossible and felt so much bigger than me. It was as if everything had lost its place in my world and I could not see how I could possibly put it all back together. I felt lost, unsure of my future direction, and confused about what I should do next.

Today, I appreciate how these, and other life changing events have helped me become who I am today. They have helped to shape me into a better, stronger and happier me, because they made me decide to make my own life happen. The events pushed me to look deeper and further than I had in the past and to dare connecting with a part of me that I had left behind. They made me decide to stop and look very closely at what mattered to me, what I really valued, what my dreams were and what I really wanted for myself.

I chose to move on from neediness and fear-based decisions to a braver, bolder and truer me who had a strong direction. To shape new relationships, friendships and even to work in ways that are so much more aligned with who I am, that make me wake up happy every day.

It was a shift from holding on to the past out of fear or confusion, towards openness, opportunity and a welcoming as to what might be coming next. This kicked off my own real journey of self-discovery and opened me to seeing the harder moments in a very different light.

Challenging life events are like wake-up calls. They force us to make a choice of either staying, clinging on to the past or to step out of the cocoon and into the real space, to face who we truly are. They force us to step up and dare a bit more; to dare to dream boldly. In fact, they force us to dare a whole lot more than we've ever done before.

Without the option of staying in the cocoon, we have no other option than to take steps we wouldn't otherwise take, to look at our self in ways we avoided before, and to see how everything takes on a whole new meaning.

I ended up redefining all I knew, loved and believed in. Every relationship I had, every activity I did, what I ate, drank, and how I lived my life just no longer felt the same. It didn't feel right, so this was my call to action! It was time to truly tune into who I was and to get to know myself on a level I had not reached before. It was time to rediscover all that strength, power and vision that had been covered in layers and layers of 'this is how we do it' and habits built up over the years.

I had forgotten who I was. I had become a part of a whole. I was no longer me and I was missing out. Breaking free was scary, and not always pretty, because moving ahead also means saying goodbye to the old. In that moment, the power lies in standing tall and saying 'next,' being fully open to allowing the new in, instead of clinging onto the past, out of fear of finding that the new isn't as good. But the new is always as good (and usually quite a lot better too) if we just allow it in.

The new, is the door to bigger and better experiences to rediscover our self, who is more fully and completely who we want to be. But, we need to decide to jump on the opportunity, to take our life further than we ever imagined possible.

We're all granted opportunities in life that we can choose to take, or choose to ignore, and the 'bumps' we meet on the road along the way, are there for a reason. It's not actually about the micro-events of the moment. It's about returning to the core of who we truly are, and the impact we wish to make across the life we choose to live. Life is intended to make us happy; and when we dare to look for that place and to claim it, knowing that we deserve it, the happiness spills over onto all the other aspects of our life.

I always suggest looking at life like a deck of cards, and to know and understand that we can choose to play our cards in the best way that makes sense to us. Focus on the hand of cards, love them and appreciate them, and decide to play them well! Know that we create all events in our life, and always remember that if one event doesn't go as planned, it's up to us to make the next one better.

Nothing ever happens to us, but always for us. What truly matters in creating our own personal happiness, is what we decide to do with each event in terms of how we choose to go on from where we are. We can't change the past, and we can't change others, but we have full freedom of choice for ourselves and our future.

Like the saying goes; 'it's never too late to have a happy childhood.' Our events in life have only the meaning that we attach to them. Events are shaped by how we feel about them, and the feelings come directly from our thoughts. So, we get to decide the level of significance we attach to our life and the events we experience. We personally have a profound effect on how our thoughts define who we want to be and it's always our choice. Events and circumstances don't define us, as they are only part of our story, but not who we truly are.

I discovered the importance of looking within, and

finding what I believe in, to realize what really matters most to me. Think about it for a moment, why does the loss of a loved one from our life hurt so much? It hurts because to some extent, we feel that we're losing a part of ourselves. It feels like we're losing a limb and we no longer feel complete. This is only a feeling, as we're still complete. When we're ready, we can always choose to return to this completeness and redefine what it looks like, to really see what it means and use the painful experience to get a much better understanding of what that means to who we are and what we are here to do.

This deep inner work can be the greatest opportunity to discover an inner strength we didn't even know we had. It can be the path to finding new levels of happiness, more opportunity than we thought possible, and a life that is so much more aligned with who we are, than what we have experienced to date. As we align our self to our own truth, this changes our entire experience of living life fully!

Life's most difficult moments are here to nudge us to focus on our truth. They are here to allow us to live the fullest life possible, the life we came here to live. This journey begins by taking a journey inside our self, to truly see and understand who we are and what we desire to be. It's an invitation to turn our experiences into nuggets of opportunity.

I dare you to ask for what will make you happy. You are

worthy of your dreams and able to reach them. What happens around you is only circumstance. What happens inside of you is potentially pure power. Life's waiting. Dare to dream boldly and create the life you most want to experience!

DORTE ERTBOLL

Dorte Ertboll is a writer, speaker, coach and mentor. She works with clients who are ready to step up, take charge of their lives, health and bodies, and to live the life of your dreams. She helps define what that life looks like, especially if you've been through major change recently or feel stuck. She helps you feel healthy, slim and beautiful, full of energy, tap into what matters, find the courage to pursue dreams, and more than anything, to find true happiness. Dare to be all you were always meant to be. Connect with Dorte at www.soul-v.com and start your journey of self-discovery.

QUESTION, EDUCATE, CHALLENGE AND CHANGE

MELISSA BOWEN

"Who am I? Why don't I fit in here?" These questions often crossed my mind as a child and young adult. Do you know the saying "square peg, round hole?" For a very long time, that was me. Have you ever felt like a square peg forced to fit into a round hole? My path to change this perception was long. It wasn't until I was thirty-one, that I was able to take a strong stance on what I believed, and how I would choose to live. Looking back, it seems miraculous as to how I became the woman I am today. It took hard work, tough choices and a lot of help.

Honestly, I didn't even realize the pattern of how it all happened until I began writing this. It is truly amazing how the benefit of hindsight can bring enlightenment. So please, let me enlighten you on how I became the woman I am today. It boils down to these key words: *question, educate, challenge, and change*. Hopefully, these words can also help you, or someone you know, as you dream boldly.

First, let me share some background. I was raised in a very old fashioned and conservative part of Canada. Options for women can be described as limited, as the expectation for women was to get married and have kids. Don't get me wrong, as there is absolutely nothing wrong or bad with this lifestyle. I just always knew it was not for me. I, at a very young age proclaimed (often loudly) that, "I am not getting married, and I am not having children!" I personally was never challenged to do more with my life than become a wife and mother, and my proclamations were often met with "Don't be ridiculous."

I was surrounded by people who often focused on the shortcomings of others, rather than their strengths. These shortcomings included being a different race, religion, sexual orientation, etc. It was confusing for me as a child, when the people around me would be supportive to people to their face, but then criticize their hopes and dreams behind their back. I was told (and believed) that many things about myself were negative; that I was too skinny, too small, too into sports, too talkative, too smart, asked too many questions, etc. This resulted in me spending a large part of my childhood "escaping" into books and sports. I would read anything I could get my hands on. I also watched as many sports as possible, basically limited to Hockey Night in Canada, playoff MLB and Canadian Football, as we only had 2 channels.

I had no idea at the time, but I was *educating* myself. I often hid my knowledge, because exposing it resulted in being told I was a know-it-all or that I talked too much. As a teenager, unhealthy escapes were added like smoking and drinking. Thankfully, I was never introduced to any hard drugs, or my life could have been very different.

Despite graduating from high school with honors, I elected not to pursue a post-secondary education. I had no idea what I wanted to study, couldn't afford to go, and quite frankly was much more interested in partying than studying. Instead, I got a job, got an apartment, and told myself, "I will go back once I figure out what to do with my life." Two years and three different jobs later, I was still in the same apartment and my life was still on the same trajectory. I was miserable, and not even aware of it. I didn't know it then, but I needed to *challenge* the belief system I was raised with, but I wasn't sure how. Thankfully, help would step in, and my life changed for the better.

The first step was actually a push. It was a day like any other. I was working at a clothing store in the mall, and my then boyfriend arrived to take me out for coffee over my break. What I didn't know is that I was about to be faced with a harsh reality check. About half way through our coffee he looked across the table at me and said, "You need to go back to school. If you stay in this town, it will kill you." I laughed it off thinking he wasn't serious. It was hard to hear someone question my life choices (or lack thereof) and tell me I needed to get *educated*. My response, was a broken, "I don't know how." Thankfully, he didn't stop there. Two weeks later, he brought me an application for the University of Calgary, and challenged me to go. I accepted, and that was the first step in *changing* my life.

I moved to Calgary, Alberta at the age of twenty-one and started University. I was surrounded by people I didn't know, with values and beliefs I had never been exposed to. This exposure allowed me to *question* the "values" I had been previously surrounded with, that were racist, sexist, bigoted, hateful and ignorant. I realized through my *education,* that many of the beliefs I had been surrounded with were wrong. I used my new knowledge to *challenge* what I was taught, and to *change* my own beliefs, realizing it is our behaviors and how we treat others, that make people good or bad.

Three years after I started University is when my life really began to move forward in a positive direction. A wonderful chance encounter shook one of my core beliefs. One beautiful night in September, was literally the first day of the rest of my life. It was the opening day of the NFL season, and the New York Jets were playing the Washington Redskins. It sounds a little cliché as I write this, but it was the day I met my now husband. The first sentence he spoke to me was "Just so you know, I think women who wear glasses are very sexy." I knew instinctively (although not consciously) that my belief of not wanting to get married and have kids was shattered.

The next morning, I realized in bewilderment that I had just met the man I would spend the rest of my life with. After three months in our long-distance relationship, I committed to move across the country to Ontario to be with him. He has been there with me through the completion of my undergraduate degree, writing the LSAT, applying for law school, moving back to Saskatchewan to attend and complete law school, articling, being called to the Bar, and starting our own law firm. To this very day, we *question, educate, challenge and change* one another to be better. It has been fourteen amazing years, and I love him and our two beautiful children more every day. I am literally the luckiest girl in the world!

My story however doesn't end here. This process to *question, educate, challenge and change* continues every day. It has resulted in some very tough decisions for my husband and I, and some with difficult emotional consequences. The most difficult so far, was the decision made shortly after our wedding to re-evaluate who we were spending our time with. Together, we *questioned* those we were surrounding ourselves with and the impact they were having on our lives. Was the impact positive or negative? We took a hard look at every person around us, and *educated* one another of the impact they were having on our lives. We *challenged* one another about our observations and beliefs. Ultimately, we *changed* our lives by removing anyone who brought only negative and drama to our lives. The result was harsh, as we cut out some immediate family members and long term "friends." We also decided to move back to southern Ontario. I now know these were the right decisions, because we are stronger as a couple, we're better parents, and better individuals. We have also been able to grow our circle of friends by only adding those who bring positivity to our lives and surrounding ourselves with like-minded people.

I am the woman I am today because my husband has walked beside me every step of the way for the past fourteen years. He is my rock, my best friend, and my soul mate. He continues to *question* me, he *educates* me, he often *challenges* me, and he most certainly has *changed* me. More importantly, he has encouraged me to *question, educate, challenge and change* myself. He has encouraged me to see the best in me.

Looking back, I may not have gone to law school without his encouragement and I certainly would not have my own practice without his support. With his encouragement and support, we are presently dreaming boldly to build a sports agency, Gladiator Hockey Agency. This dream business will effectively merge my love of law with my love for sports. I am no longer the square peg trying to fit into the round hole. I finally fit! By *questioning, educating, and challenging,* I have *changed* the mold.

I dare you to dream boldly and chase your dreams by *questioning, educating, challenging and changing.*

MELISSA BOWEN

Melissa is a wife, mother, lawyer, and sports enthusiast. She is the owner of Bowen Law Office and a Partner in Gladiator Hockey Agency. She obtained a Bachelor of Arts Degree from the University of Calgary and completed her Law Degree from the University of Saskatchewan, while having her first child during law school. She was admitted into the Law Society of Saskatchewan in 2010, and admitted into the Law Society of Upper Canada in 2012.

Connect with Melissa directly at dreamboldly@mbowenlaw.com or melissa@thehockeygroup.net.

STIR UP CONTENTMENT

BY CARRIE ROARK

You walk along a path in a park filled with trees. As you walk, you see two stones lay along the path. The first is near you. A bend at the waist is all that is required to pick up that stone. The other lay a few feet away, just off the path, behind tall grass and nestled under a log. Both are appealing in their own way, but you decide to take the one at your feet. Painted in gray letters on the stone, is one word: *discontent*. You turn it over and say, "Yes, I am so tired of my boring job."

You notice another stone nearby and pick it up as well. As you examine this one, you think, "Oh man, my husband never helps around the house." Another stone drops from a tree overhead. They're getting easier and easier to come by. This one makes you say, "I really need to get a better car." You start feeling depressed when you see yet another *discontent* stone at your feet.

You begin to wonder if they are connected. Ahh, here is the revelation! You don't have to keep these stones. You have the choice to toss them back to the ground. So you do.

You remember the other stone you first saw. You move

toward it and kneel on your hands and knees. You have to reach past the tall grass and into the nook under the log. The other stone is now in your hands. Its shape is oval. Its texture is smooth. It is a rich charcoal color with a hint of shimmer running through. On the back is written one word in spa green: *content*. You immediately feel your depression start to ease and experience a peace and a sense that things are ok now.

You put this stone deep in your pocket and continue on your way down the path. Anyone watching would notice just a hint of a skip in your step as you go.

All that stands between feelings of discontentment and contentment is a choice. Start by spending seven days with Philippians 4:8 (NIV) "Finally, brothers and sisters, whatever is true, whatever is noble, whatever is right, whatever is pure, whatever is lovely, whatever is admirable - if anything is excellent or praiseworthy - think about such things." On the first day, memorize this passage. On each subsequent day, choose one of the adjectives from the passage, such as "Lovely." Meditate on that word by making a list of things in your life that are lovely. Create a collage of lovely images, write a psalm or a poem. Repeat this exercise each day, with each of the words. See if making a choice for contentment each day makes a difference in your heart. "We must be careful not to stir up discontent; discontent destroyed them." (I Corinthians 10:10)

CARRIE ROARK

Carrie Roark is on a mission! She lived forty years stuck in negative cycles, until she learned about the power of our mindset. As an author and a certified coach with the John Maxwell Team, she'll teach you how to think about how you think. Her services are for those who long for more, but are unsure how to find it. Jumpstart results fast with a VIP day session designed to bring results quickly. Mention Dream Boldly to receive a free Power Hour. Purchase her "My Daily Focus Planning Journal" from Amazon or visit her website to live a life of intention and keep your goals front and center. Visit www.roarkcc.com.

WE DESERVE A FUTURE

BY FRANKIE GUTIERREZ

Today, I told my sister the big news! I just accepted a new career. A career that will provide a better future for my children, so that I can be the mom they deserve. I deserve this. They deserve this. We have come so far. It's difficult to imagine just how far we have come together. I'll no longer need to continue working numerous jobs, while doing all that I can to support us.

You see, I had three kids by the time I was twenty years old. Sometimes, I wonder how I'm still here to share this news with my loved ones. How did I not slip into self-destruction with drugs and alcohol when times were darkest? How is it that my children are alive and have become wonderful people?

I was told at a very young age that I would be a mom. I came from a small town where women become wives and mothers sheltered from other possibilities. I didn't realize I had other options, so I accepted that my destiny was to be a mother and wasted no time getting started.

Growing up in our childhood home, I grew up fast and filled the role as mom, nanny, and housekeeper in my family. My mother worked a lot and had her own life that didn't seem to include me. I got to see her every day, but as far as having someone to talk to, she wasn't around. If we did have the opportunity to talk, there was already so much built up resentment and anger, that I pretty much rebelled against everything.

My sister was the smartest person I knew. She was our family's pride and joy. She was super athletic, beautiful, and skinny. I was the bland one, the boring one. I had a father and she didn't, so our family overcompensated by showing her more love and support than they did me. My sister loved me, but she didn't know how to deal with me. By the time I was a teenager, the anger and resentment had set in, and I don't think anyone knew how to deal with me.

Once I had the opportunity to establish my own autonomy, I was free! It was after dark and I was with the wrong crowd. My new friends were older, careless and not supervised by adults. This led to me sneaking out and meeting Eric, my first boyfriend. Suddenly, there was a guy in my life. A guy who looked a bit like Jesus which intrigued me. He loved me and worshiped the ground that I walked on. Soon, all of my nights consisted of sneaking out of my house to be with him. At age fifteen, the combination of my drunken stepdad and the urge to escape my household, led me to moving out and staying with my boyfriend full time. He was four years older than me and worked at the time. We lived with his parents, and I soon became part of their family. I became pregnant at age sixteen, and truly met the love of my life, my son, when he was born. Eight months later I was pregnant again. I felt shamed into marrying Eric, because his family didn't want another bastard child around. I also felt like I had something to prove to my own family. Because I didn't feel valued growing up, this was my way of letting them know that I could make it without them, and that I didn't need to ask them for anything. I didn't need them at all. I was fulfilling my destiny.

I was eighteen-years-old and seven months pregnant with my second child when I said, "I do." This was supposed to be the day the fighting would stop; the day the jealousy would end; the day the name calling and possessiveness would all disappear. He promised. He promised a lot. He promised he would never cheat, never hurt me and always take care of me, but none of it was fulfilled. Instead, things became uglier. I was planning my escape when I became pregnant with my third child at age nineteen. I didn't want to procreate anymore. I couldn't manage having or caring for any more children, and depression took over. Being a wife in a very strict and old fashioned family, I did what I was told and what was expected of me.

When I made my mind up to leave, I would close my eyes and cry silently as the tears would fall. I didn't want my life to continue with my husband anymore. The more I gave, the more selfish he became, and he sucked every bit of light and existence out of me. Depression filled every hour of the day and I couldn't stand looking at my children knowing that this was the life I'd prepared for them. This was all they were going to get, nothing more. It killed me inside. I endured two more years, for a total of ten years of the abuse and madness. I began to ask myself, "Is this really my life's destiny? Is this what I want for my kids? There must be something better. Something safer."

As an excellent wife and daughter-in-law, I cooked and cleaned daily for my husband and his family. I was not allowed to go out with friends, or even have friends outside of the family. I rarely went to the bathroom alone. I couldn't take my cell phone with me to the store (the only place I could go without my husband). I couldn't go to the store without taking one of the kids. Apparently, that made my husband feel more secure. I wasn't allowed to function without my husband or his family. I am not even sure if his family knew the extent of his controlling behavior and demands. Living over a hundred miles from my own family, he didn't have to worry about their influence on me. They were no threat to him, because he had me so isolated.

My four-year-old son and two-year-old daughter had already witnessed so much, that the violence and abuse became normal for them. My husband helped our children make a joke out of me. I would get consequences like they did, and they thought it was funny. If momma gets in trouble, momma gets slapped. This had to stop. All the abuse had to stop. Would my son grow up to hurt his wife? Would my daughter also become accustomed to this abuse and be a helpless wife and young mother? I was never scared of his hand, nor the 30-06 rifle he threatened me with, but I was scared for my children. I was scared they were becoming just like him.

Prayer and God gave me strength, and eventually I broke down and confided in my mother. Thank God she understood and was with me every moment of the way. She gave me courage and strength. She prayed endlessly for my happiness and safety. I moved back home to the small town I grew up in, and started rebuilding. Now that I was in a place of peace, and my mind was clear, I started to think back to my childhood and appreciate all that had made me who I am today. My mother was an excellent provider and the hardest working person I know. She had the biggest heart and always wanted to help those in need. She taught me about God's love and how prayer heals. My Father was also a very hard worker who showed me so much love, comfort and protection. He is the one who gave me confidence and self-worth. I can't thank my parents enough for all the things, both good and bad, that have taught me well.

Eric, now my ex-husband, took every opportunity to try

to convince me that all men are the same and that I'd never find anyone better. Believe me, I wasn't in any hurry to find another! I took a year off to rediscover who I was and slowly became enamored with a tall, dark, and handsome George Clooney look-a-like fellow. He has stolen my heart, has taught me how to love myself and how to trust again. He provides for our every need, loves my children and has sacrificed so much for our happiness. He creates a happy, loving and peaceful home for all of us. Most importantly, he has helped me realize that I am worth something more than my womb. He values me, baggage and all.

My children are my greatest inspiration. Their strength, love and support have blessed me beyond measure. I've never been proud of the choices I've made, but I am very proud of my endurance. I am proud that I work hard and stand strong in the woman and mother I have become. I am grateful. Yes, I deserve a future and so do you!

FRANKIE GUTIERREZ

Frankie Gutierrez was born and raised in the beautiful mountains of Colorado. Today, she lives in Kansas City, MO, as a single mother of three children (one boy and two girls), who own her heart. She's a survivor of domestic violence and mental abuse, graduating from the school of hard knocks with honors. Her courage, along with the love and support of family and friends, have allowed her family to survive, and now thrive. Her heart has been opened wide and for the first time in her life, she finally feels free!

LIVE SIMPLY

BY ASHLEE STEPP

On a recent mission trip to Haiti, I was granted the opportunity to see life in an entirely new perspective. I looked around and saw a landscape littered with absurd amounts of trash, stagnant water, and homes with walls that were literally crumbling down. Despite the destruction surrounding them, the Haitians could often be seen worshiping God with the utmost joy in celebrating simple pleasures.

Homes were made from makeshift pieces of anything they could find, sometimes with a tarp placed over it. They were so happy and grateful simply to have a roof over their head. Children made toys using whatever they could find. For example, a toy car might be made from nothing but an empty toilet paper roll with bottle caps for wheels and a small piece of used string to pull it. Most arrived at our clinic with holes in their shoes, mix-matched shoes, or no shoes at all. Their clothes were tattered, and several hadn't seen a meal in days.

By American standards, they have nothing, yet they are so happy. One of the lessons we learned during our mission trip, is that living simply is so easy to do and so gratifying. I know that

I don't personally practice meditation or mindfulness all the time. I don't always eat healthy, but I do my best. I don't do so many of the things that can be so simple, and I would guess that many of you don't either. That's reality, because we're human right? We're not perfect, but something that is easy to do, is to live simply, and simply take care of those little things.

When we're faced with challenges in life, where can we begin? When there's a dream we want to reach, how can we achieve it? It can be intimidating to think about, but I have to tell you; it starts with the simple things. Simple things like choosing a simple nutritious food over a non-nutritious food. It doesn't have to be every single food we eat, but there has to be a balance. Simply choose to begin. Put the cell phone down and have a real conversation. Turn the television off and enjoy your family. Simply choose to see the positive things in your life and be thankful for everything. Thank the people around you. Thank the world for everything you have, because there's a lot of devastation. Be thankful for the opportunity to dream, because I can tell you that isn't an opportunity that Haitians and so many others from various countries have. Take the simple things you're granted, expand upon them and be thankful.

"Live simply" is a reminder to seek joy always. Live simply could represent a cookie-cutter home with two windows, a door, a tree outside, and sunshine in the sky. It could represent the houses in Haiti that have walls crumbling down, but joy inside. It could be that mansion on the lake with peace surrounding it.

When we arrived back to America, we were overwhelmed, because even the airport was extravagant, loud and hurried. Our dinner plate portions were heaping. For us, it was a complete reality check. We live with an excess of everything. As we were getting through customs, people were so angry and yelling. Those people didn't even realize how easy they have it. They were traveling and couldn't see the opportunity that so many will never receive.

I dare you to live in a way that you find joy in simple pleasures instead of materialistic things. Let the people that occupy your home, not the furniture that decorates it, determine your happiness. Live in a way that the blessings that surround you are in the forefront of your mind. Live simply.

ASHLEE STEPP

Ashlee Stepp is a world-changer on a mighty mission to help elevate humanity. Upon receiving her bachelor's degree in textiles, apparel, merchandising and design from South Dakota State University, she began designing her own clothing line founded on God and giving back. In addition, she's a digital designer for a global training organization and seeks opportunities to serve greater. Discover her clothing line that gives back to various global endeavors at www.AshleeStepp.com.

THE PORTRAIT OF MY TRUTH

BY CHARISSA LAWSON

As a young child, I began to develop a mental picture of what my life was supposed to be like. As I grew older, personal values and societal beliefs crept their way into the design; getting married, starting a family, and having a successful career became the focus. As I became an adult, I began to shift my emphasis on fulfilling the design; never once thinking about or revaluating if the picture I had painted for myself was a good fit or served my life's purpose.

My picture began to change in December of 2004 when I uttered the words "I want a divorce" for the very first time. Over our 11-year marriage, my husband had told me several times that he wanted a divorce. He tossed those words around as easily as asking someone if they would like cream or sugar in their coffee. It was obvious those words didn't carry the same weight and brevity in his mind, as they did in mine. Often when we'd fight, he would hurl those hurtful words at me again and again. I'd had enough. The day I fired back, "if the words I want a divorce ever leave my mouth, it will be the first and last time you will ever hear me say it." When I spoke those words on that cold December day, I felt like a failure. I was scared what others would say or think, how I'd move on with my life, what was left out there for me now that I am no longer a part of "we?" After all, I was thirty-two and had been with this man since I was seventeen; nearly half of my life. All of my hopes and dreams I had for our relationship changed overnight, but in my mind the perfect picture I had imagined for success in life hadn't changed.

Before the ink was even dry on my divorce papers, I was in another serious relationship with a man that I had known off and on for many years. Within a year we were married and settling in on our new life. I knew then, and I definitely know now, it was way too soon to start another life with someone else, when I wasn't even done recovering from the marriage I had just left. My friends and family tried to convince me to slow down and let my heart heal. What did they know? I didn't need their advice; I had already designed my life portrait and having him was key, so I kept marching on.

When I married my second husband, we both had very successful military careers spanning over ten years and we were well known throughout the Air Force community as being one of the top in our career fields. I had future dreams of becoming a Chief Master Sergeant and someday advocating for my career field. For the most part, I was well on my way fulfilling that part of the picture of success and happiness. However, it was time to start filling the children part of my portrait. We had both come from broken homes and dreamed about having children in a loving, caring and respectful environment. We both grew up in the Midwest and appreciated the roots that had been set down for us growing up. Summers, weekends and holidays were spent with aunts, uncles, cousins and close-knit friends, so we wanted the same for our children. With that in mind, we decided that being active duty would not facilitate the kind of life we wanted for our family. With a heavy heart, I separated from active duty in February of 2005 and joined the Air National Guard. My husband followed suit a year later. We moved home the following November to embrace our new lives.

About a year after we moved, we were both hired full-time with the Air National Guard. We felt blessed because we wanted to continue to serve our country, and doing it full-time without having to move every few years (like we would have had to, being active duty) sweetened the deal. Yes! I had my man, and the career portion of my portrait remained intact!

As we settled in, we began to place our focus on starting a family. We tried for a few years without success, before we finally reached out for help medically. The first step was finding out "who" was the "problem." I was convinced it was my husband; after all, my mother and my sister had gotten pregnant without any problems. I was so sure it would start and stop with him. Well it started with him, but very quickly stopped at me. However, it wasn't over from a medical perspective, so we spent the next several years, and our life's savings trying to conceive. We finally decided to stop after six years of trying. This not only took a toll on our finances, it also took a toll on our marriage. Even though my life had taken a drastic turn, I refused to alter the life picture I had painted for myself so many years before.

Fast forward to July of 2016; the marriage piece of my picture began to fall off the canvas, as I found myself about to go through another divorce. This time though, it wasn't me who uttered those words; it was my husband of 10 years. I didn't see it coming. I was frozen in shock, but I did nothing to save it. Deep down inside, I felt I deserved it. I never got over the fact that I wasn't able to give him the child that a woman was supposed to. I was damaged goods. Looking back, I wallowed in self-pity and the shame of not feeling whole; because God forbid, I couldn't bear a child. Over the years, I had become withdrawn, angry, bitter, and unwilling to engage in or acknowledge what had become my reality. I refused to shift my perspective and rework my life portrait. I lost myself and another marriage because of it.

It's taken me the better part of a year to realize that from the beginning, my picture was skewed. All these years, I had focused on what I thought was the portrait of my truth, my self-worth, and what was supposed to earn me the societal brand "successful at life." I had never really stopped to figure out what portrait was right for me personally. I just went along with what I thought I was supposed to do, and took the mechanical steps toward those goals, instead of figuring out which portrait was the best one for me.

Today, I began the journey of redesigning my portrait; allowing it to be an open canvas to forever evolve, with the grace, freedom and ease to change it as I please.

CHARISSA LAWSON

To: Mom
Charissa Lee

Charissa Lawson is a twenty-three-year veteran of the United States Air Force; with expertise in Airfield Management, Continuous Process Improvement, and life-long learning. She's supported numerous combat deployments managing airfields in Kuwait, United Arab Emirates, Iraq, and Afghanistan. She currently serves as an Airfield Manager with the 114th Fighter Wing in the Sioux Falls, SD Air National Guard. As an innovation enthusiast, Charissa is also on a mission to use her Master's in Organizational Management and Leadership Development to pursue positive change and establish relevant leadership development opportunities within her organization.

LOVE, MARRIAGE, AND OATMEAL

BY LISA GARDNER

Whenever someone in my family gets married, we simply say, "Oatmeal." What? How unromantic! Shouldn't marriage be more like a cupcake with sprinkles instead of a bowl of brown mush? Where's the passion? Where's the excitement? Where's the je n'ai sais quoi?

People usually think of oatmeal as bland and unexciting. However, it is also dependable and nourishing, a complex carbohydrate that sticks to your ribs and leaves you with a full, satisfied feeling. Oatmeal is also easily spiced up with the addition of cinnamon, fruit, and brown sugar. You can even get creative and make it more of a dessert! With this, a marriage described as oatmeal is reliable, one that you can always count on, and is good for you! You may not have extreme highs, nor deep lows, but you will have the steady assurance and calm that comes with being at peace, and knowing wherever your partner is, you are home.

For me, Oatmeal is truly romantic and comforting. My parents divorced when I was five, which wasn't the norm in 1981. It rocked my world. I went from being a vivacious little girl, to a withdrawn introvert. Fast forward five years, my mom remarried a man who was verbally and emotionally abusive. From my teenage years into my early adulthood years, I built an unbreakable wall that no one dare climb over. In high school, I never really dated; I was too broken. As I entered college, my grandfather advised me not to rely on a man, but instead to pursue a career where I could take care of myself. I took his words and ran with them, never holding a solid relationship for more than a few months. I focused on school, and then on my career.

While all of this sounds bleak to me now, I've come to realize that while my life was not all roses, the thorns I had to climb through made me tougher and stronger. I discovered I first needed to find happiness and wholeness within myself. It was a process, but as I look back, I realized that there were four steps I took.

STEP I: I FORGAVE

I had to forgive the father figure who had abused me for seventeen years. Colossians 3:12-13 addresses forgiveness. This scripture showed me that I had to clothe myself in compassion and kindness, and to forgive, just as the Lord has forgiven me. For me, that meant sitting down with a man I despised and having one of the hardest conversations of my life. I had to be real and let him know how his actions over the years had hurt me. I then had to let him know I forgave him. To be honest, I still had more healing to do because of his words and actions, but it was a start. The second part of my forgiveness came with many, many prayers to God to help me forgive. I also wrote letters to my abuser about my feelings. I never mailed those letters; they were simply a place for me to release all of my thoughts, and finish working through the healing process.

STEP II: I TRUSTED

I gave my life's journey to God. I knew it was the only way for me to find inner peace, strength and a new life. God placed my husband directly in my path during college, but I wasn't ready yet. My husband, Ray, has a different perspective about our love story. There is a whole "He said, She said" version, but what I can say with certainty, is that the man had patience; in fact, twelve years of patience! If you ask Ray, he will tell you I was a tough one. He could never figure me out!

After college, I wound up in Michigan, and so did Ray. We started out like most couples, by building a friendship. Once I knew he was someone I could trust, I made the choice to break down my wall and invite him in as a friend, rather than run, as I'd always done in the past. I simply wasn't ready for anything more. I still had more internal healing to do. So, when Ray was tapped for an overseas work assignment in China, he took it. Around that same time, I pursued a career opportunity in California. While God had the perfect man in mind for me, I needed to learn about myself first, to be open to the opportunity.

During our four years apart, Ray surprised me a couple of times and let me see the kind of man he was (and still is today). Shortly after he left for China, I went in for an emergency appendectomy. At the time, I was in a relationship with someone else, a man who chose playing soccer with his friends, over standing by my side during that scary time. Ray, on the other hand, called all the way from China to make sure I was ok. I was in shock and awe that my dear friend, Ray, had called me from overseas while my then boyfriend had better things to do. Needless-to-say, I cut the old boyfriend lose after surgery, and Ray continued to hold a special place in my heart. I later discovered that my friend Missy, had dropped Ray an email letting him know I was in surgery.

Awhile later, I mentioned to Ray that my friend and I were going to Italy on vacation. True to his caring and generous nature, he upgraded our seats to first class so we could arrive in Italy refreshed. Then he stunned me by popping up in Rome, all the way from China, to hang out for a couple of days. As crazy as it sounds now, it never registered that he had come all the way to Rome to see me because he cared for me as more than a friend. I just thought he had time to spare from work. Both these times, and others along the way, showed me how trustworthy and caring of a man he is. While I was on my own personal journey of healing, God had this amazing man waiting for me the whole time.

Four years later, when Ray returned, I had found inner peace spiritually by the grace of God, and physically through attending yoga classes twice a week. Once I found peace and happiness within myself, God opened my eyes to what had been standing in front of me the whole time, my perfect match made in heaven!

STEP III: I TOOK A RISK

I was invited to a couple of weddings that next summer, and I wanted Ray to attend with me as my plus one. The weddings seemed to be the perfect ice breakers to help me get my "feet wet" again, away from what was familiar and toward this new relationship that was slowly developing. I didn't make a move during those weddings; I was too scared. The mere fact that I asked him meant I was taking a risk. Thankfully, he said "Yes!" I did not run; I left my heart vulnerable and open to receive.

STEP IV: I TOOK ACTION

During this time, I moved from California to Phoenix. I knew I needed to take action so I did two things. First, I dropped a letter in the mail telling Ray how lucky any girl would be that married him. Understandably, he was confused! Second, while I was unpacking in Phoenix, I decided to send Ray a text by phone. We ended up texting for almost eight hours that day. Finally, I made a bold move and *said* something. I told Ray that I liked him and wanted to be more than friends! What a curve ball! He texted back that he had to sleep on it for the night, and we would talk the next day. Little did I know, my sweet man booked a plane ticket from Detroit to Phoenix for a 24-hour visit, and arrived to talk to me in person! Two years later, I moved back to Ohio, back to where it had all begun, and we got married! Ray and I agreed our friend Missy would get a front row seat to our wedding for being so kind in connecting Ray and I during my previous surgery.

God is good! He has shown me that He will provide if I put my trust in Him. He gave me a man who is honest, kind, and most of all, patient. Even with all my dents and scratches, my husband loves me for the beauty from within, not for the decoration on the outside. Today, we have three beautiful children, and my life is fully sustained. My dream to all who choose marriage, is to enter in with serene confidence.

May everyone say no to drama, choose oatmeal.

One scripture I like to refer to is I Corinthians 13:4-5, which states, "Love is patient, love is kind. It does not envy, it does not boast, it is not proud. It does not dishonor others, it is not self-seeking, it is not easily angered, it keeps no record of wrongs."

LISA GARDNER

Lisa Gardner is a wife, mother and business owner of Gardner Glam. In her makeup business, she helps empower women by helping them be their own kind of beautiful, and earn additional income using social media. Lisa loves to travel and enjoys being a kid with her kids. Interested in a consult or simply want to connect? Drop her a line on Facebook at Younique by Lisa CE Gardner.

RAIN AS BEAUTIFUL AS THE RAINBOW

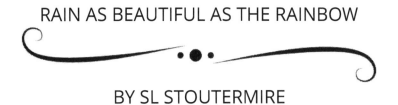

BY SL STOUTERMIRE

As a young girl, I loved to read fairytales and love stories. I enjoyed the entire story from beginning to end. I didn't just love the ending when everyone lived "happily ever after." I also loved the twists and turns the story took throughout. I realized at an early age that characters became better, upon going through the highs and lows. It's interesting that I understood that at such a young age, because it's exactly what I would recommend to anyone who's in a relationship or marriage right now.

True love is just like a fairytale. It comes with some very monumental moments; peace, joy, trials, tests, people who are supportive of your relationship, and people who are against your relationship (who will attempt to destroy it). There are always two main characters in a relationship; the two people who are in love, and trying to live their true love. The two main characters are the most important. Together, they must navigate the various stages of their love and relationship. When you enter a relationship, there's no need to rush to the "happily ever after" ending; which you may not receive unless your relationship is nurtured correctly. Every day will bring unique twists and turns into your story.

Enjoy the moments when you're laughing together (when no one else can see the funny); and be willing to hold one another tightly through the pain. Communicate openly during those moments when someone has attempted to create division between the two of you. Listen to one another as you express your feelings and thoughts about the situation. These moments will do two things for the future of your relationship, for you as individuals, and as a couple. Through the adversity, it will help you develop and strengthen your relationship, as well as your love. It will also reveal truths about the people who are surrounding you.

You need to have like-minded individuals in your life, who you can turn to for relationship advice, guidance and understanding. This doesn't need to be someone who just agrees with you, or takes your side because they are your friend. It needs to be someone willing to tell either of you the truth. Someone willing to hold each of you accountable for your part of the wrong, and celebrate the good times with you. They should be willing to be supportive during the tests, without trying to create strife and discord between you.

In relationships, you can't take advice from everyone. Someone who has never experienced a supportive relationship of love, nor been married, can't truly give you advice on your relationship. Single people can't advise married couples, because they are single. What advice can a single person offer from a true relationship standpoint? Likewise, a married couple who is miserable, and merely existing within the marriage, won't be able to offer you great relationship advice; unless it is "don't be us." A couple that doesn't believe in God, won't be praying for your relationship.

To be successful, you must be equally yoked in your marriage or relationship. Get to know each other and discuss your vision, goals, thoughts, etc. The last thing you want, is to discover two years into your relationship, that the person you're with wants to party all the time, and thinks that an open relationship is okay; while you enjoy romantic nights at home and only want to be with your partner.

Make time and space for just the two of you. Leave the woes and stresses of everyday life (that you typically discuss), behind for your special time together. Use this time to just love on each other, and celebrate your relationship. Turn off the phones, shut down technology, tune out the rest of the world and create a special space just for the two of you. You may only be able to set aside time once a week, or once a month, but make sure that you do. It's important that you have togetherness time. You don't want to feel as if all your time is spent on everything and everyone else, but then have no amount of quality time for just the two of you.

Remember to not only tell each other how much you love him or her, but show it as well. Love is an action word. Be encouraging and supportive of each other. The loudest person cheering for you should be your significant other. Do little things that may not be major to you, but are very large to your mate. Cook his or her favorite foods, surprise one another with favorite treats, finish some housework that the other person hasn't gotten around to doing, have the remote sitting beside the chair with the television already turned to the basketball game, or have the book he or she has been saying they want to read waiting for them when they get home. Most people think that you must spend a great deal of money, or do things that appear big (in the eyes of the world), for it to matter to your loved one. The truth is, it's the meaningful gifts from the heart that matter the most. This could be as simple as listening as they complain about something or someone, or having a shoulder to cry on.

Share the good times and the bad times. Sharing only the good, but hiding the bad, is ineffective. You need to openly share how you are feeling, and what you are thinking during the difficult times as well. The only way the other person will know your thoughts or feelings, is if you share them very clearly. Don't assume they will automatically know, because you don't always know what they are thinking about during the difficulties either. These are growing pains. They don't necessarily feel great in the moment, but once you've overcome them, you will look back and feel awesome, because you made it through the adversity together. It will take both of you to build and nurture a strong, healthy and loving relationship.

Take time for yourself as needed. Self-care is important. Give each other the space to do the things you may not enjoy doing with your mate. This allows you both to enjoy the simple things that you enjoy doing, and it gives you both time to miss each other; to reflect on the goodness within your relationship. Neither of you will feel crowded or as if you have to stop living, in some aspects, in order to have a great relationship. You can breathe and do things independent of each other, if it's not detrimental to your relationship. Yes, you want quality time together, but you also need quality time alone.

Things will evolve for both of you, as you deepen your relationship. You will find yourself removing people from your lives that no longer represent what you now represent, and that's okay. It's called growth. For your relationship to grow, you both must grow together as well. If neither of you grow, you may find that your relationship withers away.

I'd like to share two love notes I wrote to the other half of my fairytale.

A LOVE NOTE FOR MY PRINCE CHARMING

When I first saw you, time stood still. You took my breath away and all I could feel was the quicken of my pulse. My heart rate skyrocketed, and I couldn't take my eyes off of you. I knew in my soul that you were "it" for me. Then you, with your smooth talk, and that walk that made me sigh out loud, decided that I was your forever. You took me to heights that I had never reached. You showed me love in ways that I had never felt. You loved me, but you loved God more. After all of this time, I'm still Jonesing on you. I love you!

THE RAIN IS JUST AS BEAUTIFUL AS THE RAINBOW

I'm sitting here thinking about life, and how our journey can take so many twists and turns. I looked over at you, who is also my best friend on Earth, and I know that God truly blessed the road that lead me straight to you. It's awesome to have someone who can complete my sentence before I finish it. To have someone who can speak the thoughts I was just thinking. Someone who is proud to be a Godly man, a minister, a husband, a father, a son, and everything else God has called you to be. To have someone that will always have me. Someone that I don't mind dancing in the rain with, no matter how hard it is coming down. No umbrellas are needed because we have each other. I'm grateful to have someone who takes my breath away, and makes my heart race when he enters my mind or the room twenty years later (and counting)!

Think of your relationship as a seed that you are about to plant. You get to decide where to plant the seeds, to get the best results. Ensure that you're planting on fertile, solid ground, till the ground where you are going to plant together, plant the seeds, cover the seeds up, water them, nurture them, allow sunlight to shine down upon them, and continuously care for the seed as it blooms and grows. You must continue to care for it, and nurture it, just as you did when it was a tiny little seed in the packet that you purchased. There isn't a difference between your fairytale, your garden, and real love. All are yours to claim and live. For the rain is as beautiful as the rainbow.

SL STOUTERMIRE

SL Stoutermire lives in Alabama with her husband and seven wonderful kids. They enjoy spending time together as a family and serving God in the capacities they've been called to serve. She's committed to sharing her testimony, so that no one ever feels alone in their experiences. She's the Author of several books and publications, a business consultant, ghostwriter, grant writer, and motivational speaker who serves passionately. Learn more at www.slstoutermire.com.

A GLIMPSE OF HEAVEN

BY CINDY ABKES

My dream as a child was to be a mom someday. I wanted to get married and have children. That dream came to a halt when my appendix ruptured and I was told I would never be able to have children. I went on to marry the man of my dreams and we discovered that miracles do happen!

We were blessed with not only one, but three beautiful children; two precious girls Alyssa and Marissa, and a handsome son, Nicholaus. I couldn't help but dote over my miracle babies, capturing each moment and soaking in every memory I could with my three beautiful blessings. I chose to be a stay at home mom so I could watch them grow. I always held a fear of something happening to one of them, but placed my faith in God that they would be ok.

My deepest fear and most dreadful moment drew near when our 31-year-old son became very ill. He spent eight long weeks in the hospital. I stayed with him day and night constantly praying with him and praying over him. I prayed for God to restore his health. I wanted him to be healed and advance in his life. I was in constant prayer, day and night.

On the morning of March 22, 2012, the doctor came into his room and shared with us that the end of his life was getting near. As a mother, I tried so desperately to heal him, but I couldn't. I tried to hold myself together as I spoke with Nicholaus, as I wanted him to know that he was going to be okay. I said, "Today Nicholaus you will be in Paradise and today you are going to see Jesus." I was so choked up, I could barely get any words to come out of my mouth, but somehow I did.

We had always made a plan with our kids when we'd meet at church on Sunday's, always agreeing to meet at the right-hand side of the front doors. As I spoke with Nicholaus that morning, I said, "Nick, we will see you again and just like we have always done, we'll meet you at the gates of heaven, on the right side." He told us he'd be waiting for us.

The hours turned into minutes that beautiful spring day as Nicholaus took his final breath on Earth, and his first breath in Heaven. I witnessed my baby boy transition from Earth to Heaven. As I sat with him, I knew he fell asleep in the arms of Jesus, but couldn't help but ask God, "Why did you take my baby from me? Why couldn't you take me?" I also knew that as much as I tried to control this situation, I knew God was in control.

We spent the next few days carefully making funeral arrangements surrounded by our amazing family and friends. After the funeral was over, I found myself feeling so isolated and lonely. I desperately tried to pick up the pieces and move on, but I was completely grief stricken. I had never cried so much and had never felt so lonely. I leaned on my bible more than ever before. I prayed that God would make a path for which I could stand and walk forward on. It was so difficult for me to move into this "new normal." It didn't feel normal, as my family felt incomplete. I knew we were going to be ok. I knew God heard my prayers. I knew God had a plan for my life, but I wasn't feeling it. It was baby steps, day-by-day.

Getting from one day to the next was a great accomplishment for me. I slowly realized that God had given me time to heal from a deep heartache. I kept my faith and praised God each day, because each day was a new milestone. I was making progress! I prayed that God would use me to be a shining light in the darkest places to those who have lost a dear loved one. I made it my mission to share the good news about Christ as our savior. Heaven is real and in the blink of an eye, we will all be in Paradise.

God took our only son for His Glory and that gives me great comfort. I miss my dear sweet child daily, but the good news is that I will see him again. I am still here, to be the woman God created me to be. Psalm 34:18 The Lord is near to the brokenhearted and saves the crushed in spirit.

CINDY ABKES

Cindy Abkes is a wife, mother and grandmother who found her passion for early childhood development thirty-three years ago. She owned and operated Kids Unlimited, a childcare business, for twenty years where she was instrumental in helping parents raise 189 children across the years. She continues to pursue her passion as a substitute teacher helping to shape young minds and helps others experiencing grief. She deeply cherishes time with her daughters Alyssa and Marissa, her grandchildren, family and friends.

HE HEARS US

BY SHANNON PECK

Our daughter Ella was eleven. She had always read her bible either during the day or before bed. She often waited until I tucked her into bed to ask me about what she had read. I guess bedtime is a good time to bring up super serious stuff to discuss. She told me she needed a miracle. She read about them in every part of her bible. Why did she never hear about them in present day? She needed a miracle. We prayed she would get her miracle. Then we both went to bed.

"For we live by believing and not by seeing" (2 Corinthians 5:7)

Months go by and I am beginning to struggle physically. My breathing is labored, my energy level decreasing, and my strength declining. I would cough so hard that I would throw up. I was in my physician's office every two weeks trying to figure out the cause. This lasted from late summer to late fall. By then, I could no longer carry my then five-year-old up the stairs in the morning. I had to rest when getting to the bottom of the stairs, and then again when getting back to the top of the stairs. If I had worked on a particular day, then I would place leftovers on the counter and tell the kids to make their own supper, so I could sleep on the couch for a little bit. I could no longer run. Prior to this, I was consistently running a 5k three times per week. Now I couldn't breathe outside, and there was pain in my hips and left shoulder. Everything could be explained away. I was getting older, wasn't stretching enough, probably had allergies. My husband had been away for weeks for work and I was probably just run down.

"Be strong and courageous. Do not be afraid or terrified because of them, for the LORD your God goes with you; he will never leave you nor forsake you." (Deuteronomy 31:6)

Ella had been praying for me. She told me that God had told her that He would heal me in His own time. Of course, I was reassured. Besides, I really didn't think anything serious was wrong with me anyway. I finally felt poorly enough that I went to the ER. They knew something was up as soon as they saw me. I was put on oxygen, given an x-ray, followed by a CT scan. What had looked like fluid on my lung was now looking like a mass. A call was made to my husband, who quickly flew home (two weeks early). A biopsy followed, which confirmed that cancer cells were detected. A PT scan would later show that I had non-small cell adeno carcinoma originating in my lung. It had spread throughout my body by this point. It was on an eye, in my spine, shoulder, lung, femur, hips, neck, lymph nodes, and salt and peppered here and there. The worst part was facing my husband and parents, knowing that they had just heard the news. What was I going to say to them? What were they thinking and feeling?

Our kids came up to the hospital and reality set in. I cried as soon as I saw them. My then nine-year-old son said, "I am just glad it's not a disease that will kill you!" Coincidentally, our cat also had cancer. He turned for the worse when this was all happening. Dave and I decided to put him down right before Christmas. Amos had been our first fuzzy baby and was our surrogate child when we had gone through fertility issues. He meant so much to our whole family. Our five-year-old said to me "I don't want a new mommy." I asked her if she thought I was going to die. She said that Amos died because he had cancer, so naturally she was thinking that I would too. Ella kept reminding me that she was not worried because of what God had told her months prior.

"And so, Lord, where do I put my hope? My only hope is in you." (Psalm 39:7)

I began systemic chemotherapy almost immediately. I was told I would not lose my hair or have many of the dreaded side effects that often accompany cancer treatments. Bonus! My worries decreased, and I just let the meds do their thing. I would sleep almost entirely for days. I also tried to keep life as "normal" as possible. My attendance was crucial at classroom parties, music concerts, dance recitals and taekwondo tournaments. I was *not* going to miss a thing! I was starting to feel better. A PT scan confirmed that the chemo was doing its job and the tumors had all shrunk considerably. At this point, we found out that the cancer was caused by a gene mutation. This was good news since many gene mutations can be treated with targeted therapies, meaning there's probably at least one drug that is tailored to fight cancer cells created by a particular gene mutation. In my case there was a series of three drugs. I began the first drug in pill form which eradicated the tumors! This pill lasted about three months. The second pill last about seven months.

Cancer is pretty smart. It had found a way to work around the meds and had begun to grow and make me sick. We found out that another gene mutation was present. This is not necessarily a bad thing. This new gene mutation made me qualify for a brand-new therapy just approved by the FDA! Wow, its funny how God provides just what you need exactly when you need it! I started intravenous chemo again but with the new drug. This has kept the cancer cells from making tumors up this time. Now because this cancer is caused by a gene mutation, I will always be in some sort of therapy, unless researchers find a way to reverse the gene mutations.

"LORD my God, I called to you for help, and you healed me."

(Psalm 30:2)

Prior to my cancer diagnosis, I was busy busy busy! Three kids in activities, a husband who needs to be gone for periods of time to work, my own volunteering, and a part time job, make for a full schedule. I would often go from one activity to another, filling my day completely without any rest. Many meals would be purchased from a drive thru, and basically just poor decisions were made to save time. Often, I could be heard yelling at kiddos to hurry up, and honestly not many of us were enjoying the activities, due to the stressful schedule. Worry was captain of my ship. I was worried we would be late, worried we wouldn't be able to pay this or that, worried that I couldn't do everything. "Come to me, all you who are weary and burdened, and I will give you rest." (Matthew 11:28)

Once I was diagnosed, I wondered if anyone but me heard the wheels screech to a halt. I honestly was okay with the thought of dying, at first. I thought of the babies I had miscarried and how I would soon get to see them. Then my three earthly kiddos walked into that hospital room. Emotions ran rampant. How could I possibly leave them? I had so much to teach them and to experience with them. My husband was getting a raw deal too. Had I loved him the way he deserved? No, I really had some work to do there too. His trophy wife would have to wait. Was I good to my family? Was I a good neighbor? I fail miserably every day, but I am definitely more intentional with my time and energy. I have a new focus.

Yes, I let the meds do their thing. I also let go and let God take over. We are told not to worry. In fact, there is a verse for each day of the year saying to not be afraid. If the God of heaven's armies, the God who parted the sea, raised Lazarus from the dead, healed the blind man, turned water into wine, was raised from the dead and took my sin and sickness when He died on the cross, well then, why can't He heal me? Why can't He use my life and my circumstances to point others to Him and the exciting life and future we all have in Him? Besides, Ella needs her miracle.

"Worship the LORD your God, and his blessing will be on your food and water. I will take away sickness from among you." (Exodus 23:25)

My faith was strong. I grew up in the church. My dad's family all went to church together. We walked over to my grandparents' house after the church service or after Wednesday night catechism. My dad was a deacon and often would read a passage from his King James Bible during a meal. I, like a lot of people, strayed from the church in my high school and college years, but still believed that Christ was always with me. I remember crying to Dave in our dating years that I couldn't date someone that didn't have faith. He stuck with me even though I was clearly an emotional basket case. We decided to come back to the church when we decided to marry, and then again when we were about to welcome our first child into the world.

Getting involved became a priority when Ella was entering Sunday school. I needed to know what she was being taught. I needed to know what we would should be talking about, songs and stories I would need to remember. I continued to volunteer as my kids each entered Sunday school. The volunteering turned into a job, and now I teach elementary school aged kids each Sunday at our church. My family often volunteer alongside me. We make God our foundation. Without faith, it is so difficult to face life's challenges. I have found that it is easiest to surrender these hard times when I know that I cannot handle it myself. I may be the last person to have figured that one out. I never said I was perfect. It's a good thing I don't have to be.

"Train up a child in the way he should go, and when he is old he will not depart from it." (Proverbs 22:6)

Introducing, John Chapter 9. This passage was reintroduced to me last spring in a bible study group. It was one of those times when you re-read something, and it means something so profound for the first time. Let me tell you what it says.

"As Jesus was walking along, he saw a man who had been blind from birth. "Rabbi (or teacher)," his disciples asked him, "Why was this man born blind? Was it because of his own sins or his parents' sins?" "It was not because of his sins or his parents' sins." Jesus answered. "This happened so the power of God could be seen in him."

Then he heals the blind man to the disbelief and amazement of those who knew the man. Some didn't believe this was the same man that had been a blind beggar. The man tells everyone that the man named Jesus healed him (v. 11). Now religious leaders of the time see the man. They have two problems with this healing. The healing happened on the Sabbath (the day everyone is to rest and no one is to work) and certainly the son of God would have known about the Sabbath and would not have worked on this day. So, he must be an ordinary sinner to have done this miracle, but how could an ordinary man do this? The religious leaders question the former blind man. Then they question his parents. The parents had not seen the healing take place, so they tell the leaders that yes indeed he had been blind but now can see. The former blind man says this (v. 25) "I don't know whether he is a sinner (Jesus)," the man replied. "But I do know this: I was blind, and now I can see!" A third time he is questioned, and he says (vs. 30 and 33) "He healed my eyes, and yet you don't know where he comes from. If this man were not from God, he couldn't have done it." Sometimes our circumstances (my cancer) have to be so bad that when the healing happens, there is no other explanation than Jesus.

Once I was diagnosed, I gave control over to God. I no longer worried about how kids would get to activities or how I would make a meal, etc. I pretty much slept and did whatever I could, until I could once again participate in a normal life. I talked to God a lot, and told him the desires of my heart. I pleaded with him for years with my family, my desire to help raise my grandchildren, and to grow old with my husband. I told him how I wanted to teach kids about Jesus and his love for them.

He hears us.

Let me tell you some of what He did for our family through others. Some wonderful friends held a fundraiser for us at Pizza Ranch. So many people came that a line formed outside the door, and it was snowing! Family and friends came from near and far to help, donate and encourage. My husband's aunt sold t-shirts, and his extended family all came to church with me! Accounts were set up for us. Meals were delivered for months. Another fundraiser was held to pay our girls' dance account. Jenny wrote me a poem. Students from my children's schools held bake sales, and made me encouraging cards and games for me to take to my chemo treatments. Friends worked together to have our house painted, and another asked a local drugstore to landscape our entire yard; and they did! God went way above and beyond while taking care of us. Money, gifts, cards and food continue to make their way to our home just when we need them most. People I know, and others that I don't, have reached out to share their stories, and all of them are as incredible as you can imagine. God is moving!

"And my God will meet all your needs according to his glorious riches in Christ Jesus." (Philippians 4:19)

As I reflect, my kids are getting older, and we are all enjoying lots of experiences together. Ella has accompanied me to chemo treatments. She sees that I'm okay. She volunteers regularly in my Sunday school room, and helps teach the kids about God and faith. I tell my children and my class to dream boldly. God's plan for you will be huge! Let him do it. I don't know how long I will live. Nobody does. I have to be okay with that. His plan for my life will be so much better than anything I can dream up. He has been faithful and has shown me that he will take care of everything, no matter what. I don't know what my future holds, but I know who holds my future.

"For I know the plans I have for you," declares the Lord, "plans to prosper you and not to harm you, plans to give you hope and a future." (Jeremiah 29:11)

"He is the one you praise, he is your God, who performed for you those great and awesome wonders you saw with your own eyes." (Deuteronomy 10:21)

SHANNON PECK

Shannon Peck is married to a very selfless David and mother of three much loved children. She's a PTA Mom, a substitute teacher and professional Sunday school teacher for Embrace church. Most importantly, Shannon is a devoted servant of Christ.

GOD'S PERFECT PLAN

BY ANGELA PULSE

The bible provides examples in both the new and old testament, how He uses people to accomplish His will and purpose. This is my story. After thirty years of struggling with my purpose in life, I have finally found it, and am fully embracing my calling.

I grew up as a Mormon in Great Falls, Montana. My parents were divorced for three years when I was in my late teen years, and my siblings and I moved to Texas with my mother. My father remarried. This had a profound effect on my spiritual and academic life, as myself and all of my siblings dropped out of school for a little while. As a struggling honor student in a Texas high school, I was chosen to attend a pilot semester-long course called "Make It to the Top" with Christian leadership coach, Zig Ziglar. This had a profound effect on me from day one.

I had never been taught that success could be learned. I always thought it was an "inborne" trait for the gifted, privileged students. That course changed my life forever and catapulted me into college. While in Texas, I was still a practicing Mormon, while alternating Sunday services between Latter Day Saint (LDS) and my grandmother's Baptist church.

During my first sophomore semester in high school, I had a vision from an angelic presence with specific instructions on how to get my parents back together. Needless to say, the plan worked perfectly! My parents indeed remarried, we all celebrated together in Las Vegas, and then started a new life together in California.

Once there, I started community college as a transfer student to BYU in political science and attended the LDS Institute of Religion at the local branch church. As I was preparing for overseas missionary work and rising up in leadership within the statewide California College Republicans, I fell in love with a young man in our college student senate (government) group. I got pregnant, which catapulted me into another direction in my life at age twenty. Contemplating adoption with my mother's encouragement, I chose to keep my son, and I am so thankful today that I did. He is one of the greatest blessings to my life. My son's father moved away to the east coast and I didn't hear from him for seven years.

I was early into my pregnancy when I had another vision from an angel, that explained to me the false teachings of the LDS church and to open the Holy Bible to specific passages. So, I did. I confronted the leaders in the church with my vision, but they retorted that it was not of God and to ignore it. I could not!

Over the course of many years, I struggled being an active, but non-practicing Mormon most of the time. I spent four years in silent sexual immorality, followed by eight years of spousal abuse in a failing marriage, to a non-practicing Catholic. After the birth of my second child, I obtained my B.Sc. degree in the computer science field and filed for divorce, which split our family in half. My younger daughter went to live with her biological father, and my son stayed with me. Soon after my divorce, I met an Iowa farmer that I fell in love with, and he exposed me to organic farming in a very real and profound way. Sadly, that marriage ended a short eighteen months after it began. I found myself with two failed marriages behind me, but yet a very successful career in education, technology, policy, and agriculture.

When my son was a sophomore in high school, our lives changed dramatically again when my second divorce ended. I was dismissed from my first federal lawsuit, I obtained my M.Sc. degree, and ended that year involved in a near fatal car accident that broke my back and several other bones. Surviving that event was another encounter with my guardian angel. This was followed by rapidly being catapulted into organic agriculture leadership roles, an adjunct teaching position, key friendships with political and organizational leaders, rebaptism as a Baptist, removing myself from the LDS Mormon member records in Salt Lake, and landing a position as an international lead auditor for organic agriculture.

I then spent the following eight years traveling the world and talking intimately with God while getting educated on the plight and success of agriculture, food security, and seed supply across all corners of the world. I saw unbelievable poverty and famine in third world countries and witnessed how good technology can grow food. I spent time learning agricultural systems and technology from the Jezreel Valley of Israel to the mountains of China, to the waterways of Ecuador and even the shores of Patagonia. I dined with leaders from many ministries of agriculture and learned of their struggles, their concerns, their most intimate thoughts, and even suggestions for global policy changes and trade, as it related to seed, inputs, and organic food. I felt so privileged to learn from world leaders in the organic agriculture industry, as well as leading scholars and educators. During these years of traveling, I was blessed to purchase fifteen acres of organic land near my home, we broke ground, I became a successful organic farmer, and voluntarily opened a local food store in my hometown, in a restored historic building I owned for a short time.

Then, my mother passed away. God had been calling me home to tend to my family, and do something with all this knowledge I had accumulated. On a cold winter night in November, 2014, I arrived home from Beijing, China, feeling barely alive with the worst flu of my life, and unexpectedly my father dies of a massive heart attack hours later. While he was being transported to the hospital morgue, I was transporting myself to the hospital emergency room. I felt defeated.

These past ten years have not been easy, but they have led me to something even more profound. As I was walking through tremendous trials and tribulations of extreme degrees, I was building my story and my spiritual testimony of how God safely delivered me from the grip of the enemy dozens of times. Through illness, accident, deaths, success, and failure, I learned something from each event.

My family collapsed after my father's death, but God used me to reconcile them stronger than ever before. The relationships with my children had been ripped from my life, but God brought them back safe and sound. My parents died, but they were buried side-by-side, just as God promised me they would be; back together for always. The Lord blessed me with the greatest blessing of all, when he brought me my current husband; who is a humble, beautiful, God-fearing, prayerful man, and a devoted Christian. My husband led me straight to the body of Christ, that forever changed my entire family's life. Through trust in God, I am operating fully in His will for my life, and I better understand how and why things happened the way they did to me. I understand the full meaning of the shedding of the blood in the ultimate sacrifice that Jesus made for us on the cross for our inequities. I understand now what it means by being saved by God's grace. More importantly, I understand how the enemy operates, and I am able to use the tools that I have learned through scripture and prayer to go to battle. The victory is always His over the darkness. No matter how crazy life gets, I find peace in Jesus, and know that God is working out his perfect plan in our lives, even if we don't always know what that is in the moment.

Today, I continue to be an advocate for food safety and organic agriculture. God has stated since his initial creation of seed and animal, that we are not to create reproduction methods that He, God himself, does not see as good, which follows His ordained natural order of the universe as he laid out in His "Chain of Life." My present enemy is the restricted use of pesticide drift and GMO trespass that has occurred on my farm four times in the past ten years. This is an assault from the enemy on my right to farm organically, but also a wake-up call from God to finish the message for which he has called me to deliver.

I would like to conclude with a short message related to my future hope that Genetic Use Restriction Technology (GURT) will never be released. Monsanto has the ability to release the "terminator technology" aka GURT, which makes a plant produce sterile seeds. They are committed not to release it by their own promise. If they do, they essentially have the ability to control and contaminate the commercial food supply in the world, by producing non-seed-bearing plants. Current laws force farmers into not being able to save seed back from their harvest for replanting the next year, which has been done since the beginning of creation. It is my hope to bring forth positive change and to support and increase the production of organic agriculture, as I firmly believe our future depends upon it!

"And God said, Let the earth bring forth grass, the herb yielding seed, and the fruit tree yielding fruit after his kind, whose seed is in itself, upon the earth: and it was so. And the earth brought forth grass, and herb yielding seed after his kind, and the tree yielding fruit, whose seed was in itself, after his kind: and God saw that it was good." (Genesis 1:11-12 KJV)

ANGELA PULSE

Angela Pulse is an Educational Technologist and Program Manager of Compliance. She serves on the Natural Resource Conservation Committee for SD. She formerly served as adjunct faculty for agriculture business programs, was an international lead auditor and program evaluator for organic accreditation, executive director of the Organic Grass-fed Beef Coalition, and food safety SQF and HACCP coordinator. She owns and manages Prairiesun Organics and Prairiesun Poultry, and is launching a movement "Right to Farm Organic." She is happily married to Glenn, and together they have five children and one grandchild. Learn more @ PrairieSunOrganics.com.

MY GREATEST TEACHER

BY TOTI CADAVID

My dear son, Nick, birthed into spirit last year, just nine days shy of turning 25. Nick was only two when we learned he had a very rare condition, Primordial Dwarfism Type II, which is so rare that there are currently less than 100 people in the world diagnosed with it. Doctors predicted he'd never live past thirteen-years-old. We were thrilled when Nick passed his allotted time with us. He experienced several serious life-threatening issues, ruptured aneurisms, heart attacks, open heart surgery, etc. In total, he went through fourteen major surgeries and multiple medical procedures that kept reminding us how fragile his little body was, and how quickly we could lose him. Every time we thought the end was near, he would miraculously press on.

At the time of his passing, he was experiencing the happiest time of his life. He'd moved out on his own to live with other special needs people, where he had friends, activities, a part-time job at a manufacturing company and was in love with Amanda, his girlfriend of almost two years. He'd gotten to travel across Europe, he spent a week visiting his best friend, Brad, in

Illinois, enjoyed cousins in Oklahoma and was so proud of the two people he loved most in our world, his siblings Catalina and Santiago.

The way Nick chose to live his life and confront both his physical limitations and medical complexities made him an amazing teacher of life. This little Zen Master left us many lessons, of which I would like to share the three most important ones with you, in hopes that they may serve you as a source of inspiration.

First, Nick taught us that we must fully embrace whatever situation is sent our way with complete humility and acceptance. For Nick, everything was perfect. He never complained to God, his parents, or anyone about his size, condition, limitations, or for having so many health issues. He had all the reasons to complain, but we never heard a "Why is this happening to me?" or "Why do I have to be in the hospital again?" No matter what curveball was sent, he accepted all that he had to endure with remarkable peace, serenity and positivity.

The second lesson is that one must give oneself 100% to the task at hand, and truly enjoy the present. I don't know if Nick was like this because he knew his life wasn't going to be long, or because his soul was way more elevated than ours, but Nick truly knew how to enjoy everything to the fullest. When he spoke with anyone, he wasn't looking at his cell, or thinking about what

127

he needed to do next; he was focused on you 100%. When he spoke on the phone with his girlfriend or with his best friend Brad, with whom he spoke almost every day and sometimes for hours, he was there for as long as the other person wanted to talk. Brad shared with us that one time when they were talking, he got hungry and told Nick he was going to make himself a sandwich. After Brad made it and ate it, he came back to the phone and Nick was still there waiting for him; because they had not said good bye.

The third life lesson I want to share with you today is that Nick taught us that one must look for, and enjoy the simplest things life has to offer. Nick truly enjoyed a sunny day, a sunset, and a beautiful flower. He enjoyed a good song, a good message, a good conversation, or flavorful foods like tacos and Colombian arepas. Nick had the financial resources to buy, eat or go wherever he wanted, but instead of material possessions, he enjoyed people, memorable moments, and nature much more. For example, the Monday before his passing, he spent it outside listening to music and his audiobooks. Nick didn't work that day, so I decided to work from my home office. I went out to check on him and he said "Mommy, it is such a beautiful day, you should just work outside today. I've been outside for over six hours and I love it! I even ate breakfast outside today." So, I joined him.

As I honor Nick's life, I invite you to take these three simple, yet powerful lessons with you. Accept in your heart all circumstances in your life, so that you can find *real* happiness. Stay present in your lives, so that no-thing and no-one passes you by without fully living it. Enjoy the simple things in life. Those simple pleasures that cost you nothing, but are worth everything; such as moments with your loved ones and the moments in communion with nature.

Nick was, and will forever be, my greatest teacher. He taught me to understand that having him in my life wasn't a burden or a punishment. On the contrary, he was the greatest gift God could have ever given me. Nick didn't happen to me, he happened for me, to help me transform my life in so many ways. His love and teachings changed the way I see life and what I consider most important. Nick taught me what is worth valuing in life and how to really live a great life. The only thing I have left to say to Nick and to God is "thank you for allowing me to have him all these years. It was truly a privilege to be his mother."

TOTI CADAVID

Toti Cadavid is a seasoned multicultural branding, marketing and communications strategist with expertise in domestic and international markets. After a second near death experience, Toti went through a transformational journey to find purpose, meaning and inner alignment. She's a bestselling author, speaker, trainer, certified coach, and has launched a branding and leadership development company that helps business leaders build real personal leadership and success. Toti holds a degrees in International Business, Marketing & Organizational Development, and is certified in Entrepreneurship. Connect @ www.Ufulfilled.com or www.Essencialize.com.

MOVE MOUNTAINS

BY CARRIE STEPP

The bible shares to "Love the Lord your God with all your heart and with all your soul and with all your mind and with all your strength. The second is to Love your neighbor as yourself." (Mark 12:30-31). For me, the first part of this verse comes rather easily, but that second part has tested me fully. If you have neighbors you truly love, consider yourself very fortunate.

You see, seventeen years ago, my husband and I dreamed of finding a country acreage with a white picket fence, where horses could roam, and our kids could play. We searched for the perfect property for over three years. The moment we saw it, I knew it was the acreage I'd placed on my Dream Sheet so many years before. I'd gotten rather good at declaring bold dreams and calling them in, so our adventure began.

My husband and I started clearing trees and then built a 36'x48' tin shed in which we lived for eighteen months while we built our dream home together. Truly, it wasn't the ideal living conditions for a family, as the building materials were stored in the front, and we lived in the back, with the four of us sharing one bedroom. We both held full-time careers, so we'd work all day, grab something quick to eat for dinner, and then work on building our home together until 2am each night, only to begin again every day until our work was finished. Eventually, we had a beautiful home, all that we needed, and we were happy. There was only one problem. We continually had trials and tribulations with our neighbors.

Our neighbors owned the front forty acres, we owned the back forty acres, and we shared a driveway and a dumpster. You'd think that eighty acres would be plenty of room for the both of us, but it seemed that no matter how much we tried to tip-toe around them, how friendly we were, or how dearly we tried to "love our neighbors as ourselves," we were always being tested, and could never seem to make them happy. I'll spare you the details of all the events that took place over the years. We loved absolutely everything about our acreage, but often questioned God "why couldn't we have those so and so nice neighbors," "why does loving our neighbors as ourselves need to be so difficult" and questioned why our trust and patience was often being tested by them.

Then, the mic dropped. I had a massive digital media project underway and I'd been working tirelessly for days on end with little sleep. We'd always paid our neighbors three months in advance for the dumpster we shared. Our neighbor had called on a Monday and left a message that the dumpster fee was due.

I hadn't had a chance to get to the mailbox yet, but by 8am Wednesday morning, I'd get a taste of that sharp tongue once again. She'd called our dumpster service provider, said she was moving the dumpster, told me we had better not put one more piece of trash in her dumpster, said she never wanted to speak to me again, along with numerous other unwarranted obscenities.

Honestly, our garbage was the last thing I had time to deal with in that moment, but I made a quick phone call, ordered another dumpster and I was back to work. After a few more harsh phone calls and texts, telling me I'd better not put another piece of trash in her dumpster, I was done. It was trash, I'd already thrown it away, and there was no way I was entering into that "dumpster of life" she wanted me to enter into with her.

When my husband got home, he received the pleasure of listening to the messages and texts. That night as we drove by their home, I very clearly and boldly pointed my finger at their home and declared to my husband "that home right there will be our first investment property." Then I pointed my finger to the sky and boldly declared "God, that's my mountain and it needs to move."

I didn't know how that "mountain" was going to move, but it was time. I rested in peace knowing that all was conspiring in my favor for the greater good of all of us. To our surprise, six short weeks later, I received an unexpected phone call that began with "I need to apologize for the dumpster incident" and ended with "I was on my way home and just kept feeling that if we were in your shoes, we'd want you to tell us, so I need to let you know that we're moving, and there will be a for sale sign in our yard later today."

I know this is going to sound horrible, but you might still be able to hear my "Thank you God" as I share this. That same day, we agreed to their offer, the papers were signed, and we now own their home, acreage and that dumpster!

I'm happy to share though, that we were able to part ways with our neighbors in a very friendly manner, cleared any wrongs, and we're both at peace.

In life, there will be times when others may attempt to "take us into the dumpster" but please don't spend any of your precious time or energy there. You simply can't go there with them. Smile and wave, and let the clear desires of your heart be known. When we express ourselves with great depth of emotion and clarity, we can then rest in peace knowing that the lessons intended to be learned will be received as gifts.

On the other hand, my husband should have been a bit more clear in his intentions. Over the years, he'd casually say "I'd like to own a home in the south one day." Well guess what? Both of our wishes were granted! God moved my mountain, and our neighbor's home is planted precisely south of our present home, so my husband now owns his home in the south too!

I'd like to introduce you to the vibrational scale of emotion. Take a moment to get a sense for how you're feeling right now. Can you identify where you are in the cup? Is your cup overflowing, or is it running on empty? The more often you can align with what I call the "God frequency" or "Divine Love" frequency of 528 Hz or above, the more miracles you'll experience. Move through your day with love, joy and peace in your heart, and then watch for the synchronicities and miracles to come pouring in.

Along with this book, a key is being granted for you to unlock the eLearning course "Manifest Miracles OnDemand" by visiting DreamBoldly.org to experience more tools such as this one, being designed to help guide you as you dream boldly.

VIBRATIONAL SCALE OF EMOTION

Emotional Frequency	Thoughts - Motivation
700 + Enlightenment	Peace - Metaness - Well Being
600 Peace	Welcome - Exhilaration - Abundance
540 Joy	Empathy - Inspiration - Clarity
528 Divine Love	Gratitude - Devotion - Generosity
500 Love	Cooperation - Trust
400 Reasoning	Amusement - Curiosity
350 Acceptance	Discovery - Challenge
310 Willingness	Duty - Obligation
250 Neutral	Nervous - Worry - Hyper
175 Pride	Confusion - Annoyance
150 Anger	Rage - Defiance - Boredom
100 Fear	Threat - Hate - Blame
75 Grief	Depleted - Loss - Burden
30 Guilt	Resignation - Depressed
20 Shame	Apathy - Helpless - Death

CARRIE STEPP

Carrie Stepp is the Creator of Dream Boldly. As a global thought leader specializing in transformative personal and professional development, she's on a bold mission to inspire, heal and empower the world in which we share. She's a Midwestern country girl that's full of heart & branded in technology. Master Teacher is her life's purpose. She's invested 23 years as an Award-Winning Master Course Designer, Inventor, International Best-Selling Author and Intuitive Creator who guides leaders in bringing their dreams to life in living color. Learn more at CarrieStepp.com or email Carrie@eLearningSuccessCoach.com.

ALIGN WITH YOUR SOVEREIGNTY

BY SAMANTHA BEARDEN

Twenty years ago, I had my DNA activated and it was one of the best decisions I've made. DNA Activation is the marrying of your physical DNA strands to your etheric strands that opens you up to heightened possibilities and perceptions. I learned the foundation of DNA Activation, but then walked away from it in the 90's out of uncertainty.

Years later, I received a vision, and was told that I would be activating DNA to the masses and I thought, "No way. They have the wrong person, as there's no way I could shoulder that." In spite of myself "running away" (because you never really get to run away from your calling, as it will hunt you down).

I was slowly able to see the emergence of my healing abilities. Even with all the other craziness I was up to at the time, I studied and implemented various spiritual practices under natural healers and shamans. This included kinesiology, which is the transfer of energy to heal dis-ease in the body. Energetic misalignment manifests as physical maladies. Kinesiology corrects these energetic misalignments. I knew this was the healing modality meant for me, so for the next twenty years, I helped people with their emotional and physical health.   I began to feel as though there was more I was meant to do, something much greater than myself. I just couldn't put my finger on what that was. I wanted to heal people in a much greater capacity, to help them on a grander scale and help them remember how to heal themselves. This was all I could think about.

At this point, my life became challenging. I left my job and my marriage to the one I "knew" I was going to be with forever was failing. Somewhere deep within, I could still feel the stirring, and knew something greater was coming. This is when I was introduced to the Sacred DNA Restructure Method®.

One night, something woke me up, and I was in a state that hovered between consciousness and unconsciousness. Words flooded my mind, and a download was received that I promptly wrote down, as I somehow knew how important the message was for me. The next morning, I glanced at what I'd written. It was the exact download for the Sacred DNA Restructure Method. I saw exactly how I would help people step into their sovereignty, and remember their birthright as being *The Creator* of their lives. I wanted to celebrate, as I knew how important this was for humanity!

Then, unexpectedly my three-year-old son, Kingston, broke his femur (the hardest, densest bone to break) while doing a

Ninja Turtle move gone wrong, while playing with his dad.

At the hospital, I watched him lie on the bed in pain. He was confused and scared, while doctors and nurses came in and out. Sadness washed over me. I was afraid and felt lost. I worried about Kingston, because out of my three kids, he was the first one to break anything. I went from being on this amazing high to heal the world, to crashing down face first. I also knew that things like this can (and often do) happen when something huge is about to occur for our life. It's like the universe saying, "Let's see how you handle this, because something much greater for you, is on its way, SisStar. Do you want to continue living a life half lived or play it out fully?" I, for sure, wanted to live it out fully, as that's my jam!

As we sat there in the hospital with Kingston, I meditated and asked my spirit guides what I should do. I was told to activate his DNA. The problem was, I'd never actually activated or restructured anyone using the method I'd been given yet. Needless to say, I was a little nervous. This was my baby! What if I failed and messed him up somehow? Just then, exactly as the DNA Restructure Method® had shown up for me, I received another message. My consciousness shifted and all the doubt fell away. I gave myself permission to open my mind, and the work came forth.

That day, September 12, 2015, I activated Kingston's DNA,

and followed it up with the restructuring method I was shown a few nights before. The next day, Kingston was released from the hospital in a full body cast, with a bunch of care instructions. We were told to bring him back in fourteen days. Due to complications in his full body cast, we needed to return in ten days to get a new cast. Before the new cast was placed, the doctor decided to do an x-ray.

We waited for what seemed like hours for Kingston to return, and for the doctor to talk with us. When we finally met, the doctor said, "You're not going to believe this, because I hardly do." He showed us the first x-ray of the break, where we could clearly see the snap. He then compared it to the new x-ray, where we could barely see the break anymore. The bone had fused itself almost instantaneously. The DNA Restructure Method® had worked, and my son was living proof! The doctor was astonished and said that he would have let him leave without a new cast, but he was afraid it'd be seen as negligence, and could be kicked off the board if he didn't.

Because Kingston had no misaligned energy blocking the activation, his healing was almost instantaneous. His x-rays confirmed to me there is a diamond mine locked within the DNA, that activation and restructuring unlock.

With this, I'm now activating, restructuring DNA and healing the masses, exactly as received in the visions. This method helps people access true miracles. My life has expanded, and so has the lives of so many! There's no reason to live a life half filled. It's time to shatter those glass ceilings and step into your sovereignty!

SAMANTHA BEARDEN

Samantha Bearden is the mom of three (The Fabulous 3), Star Shaman, and the Sacred DNA Restructure Method® Creatrix. She activates and restructures human DNA energetically, so that everyone has the opportunity to excel in the game of life, using their own unique talents and gifts. She connects with biblical teachers and galactic connections within her New Orleans ancestry, to bring to life the magic within. Learn more at www.SamanthaHeals.com or connect to her Facebook group Abundance Flashmob.

AN INFINITE BEING OF PURE LIGHT

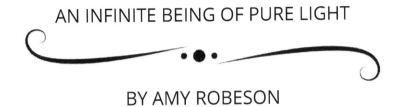

BY AMY ROBESON

I grabbed the knife off the kitchen counter and stood there looking at it. Tears were rolling down my face, blurring my vision and I didn't know what to do. The sadness I felt was more than I could bear. There was so much sorrow and so much loss. I wanted it all to end. I wanted my life to end. It would be so easy to do it. Just one move with that knife and it would be all over. Darkness would descend, and I would never have to deal with the reality of my existence, ever again.

I lived in a home full of anger, hurt and pain. My stepdad was a raging alcoholic. My mother worked almost all the time and my two sisters and I were often left alone with him. Deep down, I knew why my mom worked so hard. It was the same reason I'd picked up that knife; she wanted to escape.

Growing up, Mom wasn't formally educated, and for the longest time she couldn't even read. She found her way back to school as an adult. Then, she worked her way through nursing school because she was determined to provide for me and my sisters. She wanted us to have a different life (a better life) than she did.

When my Step-Dad entered our world, everything was wonderful until he started drinking heavily every night for years. The more he drank, the more we feared him. He was a deeply unhappy man, and the smallest things would send him down a destructive, violent path. We walked on eggshells all the time, praying he wouldn't get upset. Praying he wouldn't turn on us. Praying he wouldn't start the verbal, emotional and physical abuse.

I remember the endless feeling of hopelessness that cast a shadow over my life at that time. I was so afraid he would beat me, or yell at me, but most of all, I was terrified he would start to touch me again.

He'd sexually abuse me when my mom was at work, and even when she was at home. He'd wait until she fell asleep, and then he'd look for me. This continued for a long time, and I didn't think it would ever stop. I was only fourteen, and I didn't know what to do, or who to turn to. He told me if I ever told anyone, he would kill himself. As much as I hated how he treated me and my family, he was still the only father I ever had.

I eventually convinced my Mom that she would be okay if she left him. The sexual abuse I hid for a long time. I was ashamed of what happened, scared of how my mom would feel, and what my step dad might do if I told her. Even after I moved out on my own, the sadness and shame from the abuse followed me around like a black cloud, and I couldn't take it anymore. The only way I thought I could end the sadness was to end my life.

So, there I stood in the kitchen staring at that knife in my hand. Ready to do what I needed to do to end it all. I took a deep breath and that's when it happened. A new thought entered my mind. It was a revelation; an epiphany. I suddenly realized that if I took my own life, I was admitting defeat. I would be the wounded one. The one who lost everything.

I would be the victim.

When that awareness came to me, something stirred deep inside. It felt like I was waking up after being asleep my whole life and I was certain of one thing. I didn't want to be a victim. I wanted to be the woman who transformed her sorrow into joy, and her pain to power. I put that knife down and I started making changes.

I began to give myself what I most needed and wanted. I gave myself permission to be happy, and to look for love and goodness all around me. I found joy in little things like the gentle warmth of a summer breeze, or the sound of birds chirping outside my window. I started to read spiritual books, and to consciously connect with Source. I discovered who I truly was under all that pain and abuse, and I slowly healed my wounds by exploring all my hurt feelings and emotions. The more I bravely faced my pain, the more my life changed.

I believe we all have experiences from the past that hurt us so badly we can't even think about them, without feeling like we're drowning in a sea of pain and sorrow. We don't want to go there. We don't want to explore those feelings to shine a light on those dark places in our minds, but that's exactly what we must do.

We can't erase the past, but we can be brave and explore our feelings and emotions around those painful experiences. When we do, we completely transform our reality in the present moment, and empower ourselves to create a beautiful future.

My decision to put that knife down, to step into my power and face my pain, changed everything for me. It was the first time I empowered myself to choose a different life. It was the first time I made a conscious decision not to be a victim of my circumstances.

Today, I have peace in my life where I'm free of my past and the stories that came with it. I am not a victim. I never was. I am an *infinite being of pure light* and so are you. We all are! We don't have to discover who we truly are, we just need to remember. As a healer and a coach, I'm dedicating my life to helping people remember this divine truth. This is the truth that empowered me all those years ago. It's the truth that set me free. It's the truth that will set us all free.

Always remember that you are the keeper of your happiness.

Don't ever let anyone dim your light.

You are an infinite being of pure light!

AMY ROBESON

Amy Robeson is a gifted healer and spiritual business coach. She integrates proven business strategies with the infinite power of spiritual healing and energy work, to help her clients create aligned, profitable businesses. Amy is also a skilled teacher with a rare ability to clearly communicate high concept spiritual and business knowledge, so her students become successful entrepreneurs and powerful healers in their own right. Amy is devoted to reconnecting people to their innate divine nature, so they can experience more joy, abundance and love in their lives. Connect with Amy at www.awakeninglifecoaching.com.

BRIDGE TO BLISS

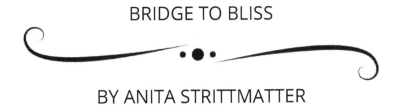

BY ANITA STRITTMATTER

Do the Hustle! Wouldn't it be great if I was referring to the song? Unfortunately, too many of us are living our lives chronically, instead of dancing with it. All too often, our mind-body connection is screaming to get out; but unfortunately, we often have no idea how to release it, even if it's killing us!

At one point, I was so bogged down in the race of my hustle, there was no such thing as strolling out to the dance floor either. You see, I used to be a real estate investor. I built homes, updated fixer-uppers, revitalized rentals and sold homes. The upside was that I loved designing floor plans that were functional and beautiful. I did so well that other investors in my city copied my ideas! The downside appeared when my contractors stopped doing what they were paid and contracted to do. So, I was forced to fire them, rehire new and begin again.

All was well at first. Then, it started happening again. This time though, I was in deep. I had no more wiggle room in my finances. Six major rehabs were in process, they were all behind, and I was pressing closer to my loan deadline.

Pressure, under pressure! Yes, another song comes to

mind. I didn't know what to do, yet the song and dance continued. It wasn't blissful; it was stressful. I began showing up on the job site to paint and do all that I could do. Seven days a week, I woke up at 7:30am, worked all day, and went to bed around 11:30 for about ten months.

I was very stressed, had no work-life balance, and had one day off for Thanksgiving. What a glorious Thanksgiving that year was! I never appreciated Thanksgiving more in my entire life.

It didn't take long before my body started showing signs of how detrimental the ongoing stress of this relentless hustle was. I developed pain I had never felt before, that only seemed alleviated when I sat down or squatted.

Being someone who believed in choosing the natural, holistic treatment model first, I visited a holistic doctor and we ran the diagnostic tests. When they came back, it revealed I had endometriosis and endometrial cysts. It was the cyst pushing on a nerve that was making it hard to stand. My doctor made lifestyle prescriptions, and I started seeing an acupuncturist who specialized in resolving feminine issues. With their guidance, the cyst was shrunk by about 25/30%.

I was elated! But then, not only was my acupuncturist moving to Europe, but I ran out of money. Things got so bad, I had no money to throw anywhere at anything. I couldn't support my own health, and I couldn't keep my projects going any more.

I attempted to sell my properties to other investors as is, but because we were on the precipice of the 2008 housing market crash, the banks were in denial. They wouldn't take any deals, as the investors knew there was no way to properly value anything. Needless to say, with nothing selling and no money, I lost everything; my business, my home, my car was returned to the bank, and my healthy worsened.

Awhile later, my boyfriend and I started a new rental real estate business. I couldn't believe that I was diving back in so soon. As the years went on though, my pain got so bad that I couldn't even pick up my kitties.

It wasn't long before I couldn't sleep any more. It was then, that I knew I was at the end of this journey. I knew through all the struggles I had endured for years, the only thing I had going for me was that I could sleep, but now I didn't even have that. Every time I moved in my sleep, I would wake up from the pain, and I knew it was the beginning of the end.

With my deep belief in holistic healing, I wanted to try one last thing before surgery. I reached out to my friend who had a wonderful experience with his chiropractor, and made an appointment. This man, Dr. Cooper, was absolutely brilliant! He is literally an enigma in his field, and cared for me as a whole-being, not as individual parts and pieces. You can imagine how deflated I was after a thorough examination, when he told me he wouldn't touch me until after I had surgery! My hope was gone. If a holistic doctor who worked in a German women's clinic for ten years was telling me he never saw anyone heal from this situation, it was time to succumb to the surgery.

Recovery was very difficult. I had never been through anything like it before, so I didn't know what to expect. At times, it seemed like I was getting better, and then it would get markedly worse. By the time I had my seven-day post-op checkup, I could barely walk. Even strangers on the street were asking to help me. My doctor looked at me and said, "Anita you need to go back to the hospital." I said, "When?" He said, "Now!" I knew he was right, and completely gave in.

As it turned out, I was going septic. I was very close to dying, and lucky to have gotten it before it got me. They began pumping me full of approximately eighteen different kinds of antibiotics. Thankfully, it worked. It saved my life and four days later I was able to go home.

While the recovery was long, I began to assume more and more of my real estate responsibilities back. We were having problems with our tenants destroying the houses and not paying the rent. Once again money strain was a concern.

Here I was yet again; except this time, I was fighting my then boyfriend to take the breaks I needed so badly. I had been down this road. I knew it didn't work for me, yet I couldn't get away from the pressure I felt from him. So now, there was a new challenge, my mindset. I was becoming very, very bitter; and I had never been bitter a day in my life.

Albert Einstein is famous for saying "We cannot solve our problems with the same thinking we used when we created them." I realized I needed to make a shift, as I could no longer live this way. But what would I do? I knew I loved holistic health and healing, but that was so broad. I packed up my kitty and went to the beach by myself for a few days, with the intention of eating healthy, doing yoga, sleeping, reading books, meditating, and all around having time to myself. This was just what the doctor ordered!

It was what I needed then, and it was exactly what I needed now; a change of scenery, and time away from the constant hustle to allow for creativity and connection with myself to flow again.

I began to listen! It makes me cry as I share this with you. I said, "God just tell me what to do. I know whatever you tell me to do will be better than anything I come up with. So, you tell me what to do and I'll do it."

God said clear as day, "Svaroopa Yoga." What? I had just gotten home from a Svaroopa Yoga class, otherwise I wouldn't have known what that was.

I asked again. God said, "Svaroopa Yoga." I said, "Really?" She said, "Yes."

Not only was this the most brilliant decision for me to activate healing in my own well-being and remedy the pain caused from surgery, but all the other pains from my athletic days and past injuries too. Moreover, as I decompressed and released the core tensions in my spine, my mind and emotions became much calmer too. My awareness, inner connection, intuitive inspirations and realizations flowed. I was more grounded, less reactive and more responsive. My natural state of joy and positivity came back. I actually liked being around me again!

Not only did I feel better, this journey propelled me into a new, more fulfilling career. It felt so amazing to share because it was so effective, and worked reliably and comprehensively on a mind-body-spirit level. Over the years, I've been able to empower other people too; even those with thirty or more years of daily chronic pain. I'm helping people release the pains and dance with life again! As you can imagine, this is a game-changer!

Now we all know there are times when things simply need to get done, but living continuously in this space literally sucks the life force out of every cell in our being. It creates physical, mental, emotional and energetic resistance.

Resistance creates tension. Tension creates pain, stops flow, and pulls our life out of alignment.

It's time to cross this bridge to bliss; to be bold enough to listen, melt and release the resistance. Allow ourselves to recreate the absolute bliss of ease, balance, and harmony in our whole life, so we can dance once again with our dreams, and see them come true.

ANITA STRITTMATTER

Anita Strittmatter is a Bliss Inducer. She guides her clients to transcend the unsustainable hustle, release physical pain, and internal resistance so that ease, harmony and balance are restored again. Drawing upon her Kinesiology degree, thousands of hours of study as a Spinal Decompression Yoga Therapist, and other self-development tools, she works miraculous wonders, both remotely and in-person with VIP retreats. Her clients experience relief in their bodies and a centered mind that transcends them from resist to bliss. Connect with Anita @ www.facebook.com/AnitaChandraYoga

REMOVE THE REEL AND KEEP IT REAL

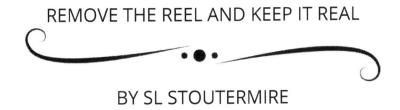

BY SL STOUTERMIRE

Life has its way of walking us through the teachings, learning and growth meant for us; even if we're being dragged through it. With it, comes pains, hurts, healing and forgiveness. I'm here today, to share with you the process I went through. I won't deny that it isn't easy, but I believe you're worth it.

In order to release and heal from the old, I first had to get rid of all that held me back from walking in the calling that God has chosen for me. It's a process, but my desire positioned me for the purpose God has gifted me. I'm about to share a bit of this journey, to remind you of your destiny.

Along my walk, there have been many people and things that wanted to take me away from my purpose anytime I allowed myself to get distracted with the chaos and confusion. This increased the moment I started to turn my life over to God fully. It was always there. It just became more visible in every aspect of my life. This is how the enemy operates.

First, I had to remember that the destiny that God has for me, is truly too great to give up for anything. I'm a living testimony! Don't allow this world to take away from you all that

God has for you, and don't allow your flesh to give it away.

Next, I stopped thinking I could fake it until I made it. I could put on all the makeup I wanted, to try to cover up my problems; but makeup fades. As it fades, it reveals the true me, along with all my problems. I dare you to accept that there is madness behind that makeup. It may be relationship madness, financial madness, spiritual madness, employment madness, friendship madness, etc. If you're not feeling as though you're being tested in some way, you may want to dig deeper.

I dare you, as *real* people, to turn off the movie *reel* and stop pretending you don't have *real* problems. Allow yourself to ask God to seek and unveil your *real* for you! This allows you to discover the real you, underneath all that cover up. Once you start to find the real you, then you can truly start to go to God and ask Him to help you find you (in your entirety). As long as you are pretending, you will never get to the real you, nor the real purpose God has for you. So you have a choice to make. Do you want to live for this world or for Christ? It's time to remove the reel, and keep it real!

As I've walked my spiritual journey, I needed to accept that some people only want the spotlight on them. These people can't help us grow spiritually, because they are still living in the flesh. They crave it. They can't be happy for me, nor anyone else for that matter, because they're often filled with misery. Even our trials become about them. They love the show, but aren't interested in doing the work. They might say they're there for you, but you'll never see them. They call themselves "friends" and say the right things, but truthfully, they are full of envy and self-hate.

You see, the life they thought they deserved is the one that God had blessed me with. They decided a long time ago that my potential wasn't great, so they wrote me off in their mind; even if they never said it to my face. But God! They can't understand why they don't have everything they thought they deserved. They can't truly celebrate my blessings, so they pretend to be happy, but put out subliminal messages that tell the real story. As God revealed these people, I didn't get upset. Praise Him! He has just told me that it's time to take some weeds out of my garden, so that my harvest isn't affected or overtaken by dead things!

My next step was to deal with the strongholds within me, that I projected outwards toward others. These strongholds caused me to lose my own way, because I lost focus of my true goal; which was to be in the designated place or position that God has called me to be. I couldn't walk in my purpose for Christ, and held on to these things, that I was meant to let go of.

While this message is for everyone, I want to speak to women directly for a moment. Ladies, some of us seem to suffer from spirits of competitiveness, envy, anger and spite. We want what other women have in their lives, or what we view as that woman's standing in her walk. We refuse to support each other. We can't wish each other well, because we're secretly wishing each other hell. We become angry if another woman is blessed to do something in her life, that we feel we wanted to do. We attempt to sabotage another, just to feel an evil sense of satisfaction at watching another woman fail.

Here's my advice to anyone suffering from this state of contempt. First of all, I'd suggest talking a long walk, and talk with God! Secondly, I want you to understand this; while you are coveting that woman's life, you better understand that she went through her own hell to get to where she is today. Her journey wasn't easy, but she pressed on because of her faith in God. When it felt like tornadoes, hurricanes, tsunamis, torpedoes, and every other kind of disaster (trials) were tearing her apart and attempting to destruct her, she pressed on. She stumbled and fell, but she didn't lay there and wait on those disasters (trials) to pass her by. She called on the Lord and He heard her cry.

She arose with determination and a desire to make it out alive! She didn't look around to compare her life to that of another woman. She didn't begrudge others of their success. She cheered them on, even when her own spirit felt lack. Not one harsh word did she utter against another, to make herself look better. She understands that she isn't called to correct. God will handle that in His own sweet time. Before you decide you want her present, you better want her past! You don't get to cherry pick the good, and leave the bad. It's all or nothing Honey.

Women are not your competition. Your competition is "day" and "self." On Sunday, Monday, Tuesday, Wednesday, Thursday, Friday and Saturday, you're competing with "day" and "self" 24 hours a day, 7 days a week. You're competing with "day" to ensure that anything not of God is left in the past, while you prepare for your present (a gift) and your future! You're competing with "self" to ensure that you're aligning yourself with God daily, and that it's His will you're following and not your own. Remember that when you covet what another person has, you are essentially telling God that what He's doing and has done for you isn't good enough.

Once I accepted that people pleasing wasn't my focus (nor my purpose), I gained a new sense of freedom. God is the only one I want to hear say, "Well done, come in my child." I set myself free from the constraints of worry, how others viewed me, and know this world is not my home.

When I was younger, I would hear my Uncle Joe (who is at rest) say, "When I die, don't cry for me. Don't cry for me! Why are you crying for me? I'm going home to be with the Lord! I feel sorry for you all. You all will still be here." He always seemed to be at peace, and excitedly taught about the Lord. There was something about him that always rejoiced within his spirit and you could feel it. As a child, I could see it! His teachings still resonate with me today. I can still remember him standing at the church podium. I can see that smile on his face and I can hear him as he taught. I never fully grasped what he meant when I was a little girl, but I knew there was something better than this world to look forward to.

Through the years, my relationship with Christ has grown and strengthened. My understanding of The Word has become clearer through the Holy Spirit. My walk is Christ centered. My life is not my own. As I reflect on all that my uncle taught me, I thank God because I understand now. When I think of 2 Corinthians 5, I cry and I smile. I cry because I fully understand what he meant! This world is not my home. I smile for the same reason! This world is not my home. I will go home to be with the Lord! Hallelujah!

Based upon my own understanding, I've declared to set aside personal judgements toward others, because I don't know their story. I don't know what caused them to be who they were in that moment. Yes, "that moment," because aren't we a living witness that Christ can change anyone? Every day, people are condemning others for their actions, ways, lifestyles, comments, living environments, their past, etc. I just want to ask you one question. Do you know their story? It's easy to stand in judgment when you've been standing on the sidelines the entire time; but do you know their story? How many times have you seen them get knocked down, only to rise again? I hear people say, "I lived right next door to them. They didn't go through anything." "They had parents who loved them." "They had everything they could want in life."

Let me share something with you. Unless you were that person, you don't know what others have gone through in their lives! How much domestic violence did they witness in their homes? How often are they still waking up from nightmares from the horrors of their childhood? How many had a mother tell them she never wanted them? How many had a father try to rape them? How many know what it's like to eat out of garbage cans or live in homes with no utilities? How many never had a mother to share what mothers and daughters share? How many had family members who knew, but didn't stop it? How much self-hate are they living with internally? How many lived with insecurities that are still manifesting in their lives today? How many have received help but are still emotionally and mentally scarred?

How many were written off before they could even begin? Some may read this and think you know your "enemies" well enough, but you can't even begin to imagine! Don't you dare judge what you can't possibly understand! And, if you decide to seek revenge, prepare to dig two graves.

The most difficult book I've ever written was my first one "Strength: It's What I Found When I Removed My Makeup." Why? It required that I share some of my life's story, to help others understand that it's okay to not be okay! I was liberated from a place of wanting to help and not condemn. I can no longer stay silent. There are too many people hurting. We need healing! God calls on us to help one another, not to cast stones at another. Do you know their story? If not, don't be so quick to judge!

In closing, I want to remind you of this scripture. "And we know that for those who love God all things work together for good, for those who are called according to his purpose." (Romans 8:28). I've read this verse many times. I've said it to myself and others, but it's amazing when the Holy Spirit gives you guidance and clarity on The Word. Yes, the first part does say, "And we know that for those who love God all things work together for good." This is very true, but we can't stop reading there. We must go further into that verse and to be sure we don't miss everything God said in that verse. The second part of the verse says, "for those who are called according to His purpose." Wow! Those who are called according to His purpose; not the purpose we decide on; not the purpose that yields the most money, fame, fortune or friends, but according to His purpose. I pray that each of us explores this verse. I dare you to live it. Stay blessed!

It's so important to focus on the "real," not the "reel." Just because something looks pretty on the outside, doesn't always mean it's "real." That pretty flower could be poisonous, so make sure you're planting flowers and not weeds. As I've grown wiser, I've trusted God to weed my garden of the people and things who have no place, and serve no purpose, from the life I have from Him. Today, my circle looks different and it's a great deal smaller now that God has taken over. I find peace in knowing He truly has the best plans for me, so I trust Him over my life. I've been reminded not to replant the people or things that God has already removed from my garden of life. Weeds in my garden will affect my ability to work the garden, as well as the harvest of the garden. It doesn't matter if the weed is big or small. If I leave it in my garden, it will eventually spread and overtake the plentiful harvest. Sometimes we can't see the harvest, because there are too many weeds in the way. Your harvest is waiting for you when you're ready! Dream boldly and prepare to receive!

SL STOUTERMIRE

SL Stoutermire lives in Alabama with her husband and seven wonderful kids. They enjoy spending time together as a family and serving God in the capacities they've been called to serve. She's committed to sharing her testimony, so that no one ever feels alone in their experiences. She's the Author of several books, a business consultant and motivational speaker who serves passionately. Learn more at www.slstoutermire.com.

YOU'RE NOT FINISHED HERE YET

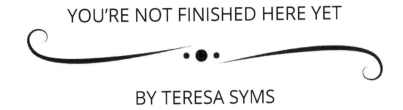

BY TERESA SYMS

Faith has always played a massive role in my life. For example, I believed in living by the rules, being good to one another, treating people well and above all, loving one another. It took me many years to understand what my faith truly meant, but awakenings can happen at any given minute for a multitude of reasons, and usually when you least expect it.

I did not understand until just recently that my entire life had purpose. All the traumas, abuse and brutality that I have survived were given to me as a life journey that I had to endure for God's plan. He had something in mind for me, and like all human beings, we constantly ask why.

My family is originally from Belgium. My grandmother as a young girl was forced to come to Canada in 1925 to work on her parents' tobacco farm as their hired man. Up until 1960, tobacco farming was all my family knew. They were hard working people who had no idea how to love their children or themselves. Work was all there was, and believe me, it was back-breaking, hard, filthy work.

I was the fifth child for my parents, but only the second

live birth. My three older brothers were still-born, sending my already emotionally delicate mother over the deep-edge many times. She found some comfort finally when my older sister was born. She had a child, she was content, happy and lost in her own world of insecurity and mental illness. My father found other ways to cope with his own unfulfilled life. He was an abused child, who worked long hard hours for his parents on the farm. Other than being physically beaten by his father, his main source of anger and shame was being raised in a small farming community, where everyone believed he was a product of incest. My father found life difficult to manage and became an alcoholic. He was unable to numb the pain and shame of 'incest,' or the fact that his turn at tobacco farming ended in 1959 by bankruptcy, just before I was born. My parents lost everything and had to depend on my other grandparents' rental properties to provide us with a home.

My sister, a self-centered, spoiled, only child, was happy (until I was born). I needed a great deal of care for the first few years, as I was born crippled from clubfeet. My legs were straightened immediately but for two years, I wore braces with a steel bar between my feet. You would think a tiny cripple baby would be loved and well cared for. I was the exception. My mother constantly told me as I grew up that I was not wanted, never was and never would be. I never understood what I had done to deserve this.

After I learned to walk, I rarely sat still. Growing up in a dysfunctional home was a challenge, which I probably could have survived easily had it not been for the horrific abuse my father inflicted upon me during his drunken rages. His favorite form of punishment for me was to have me kneel, bare kneed for hours, on beer bottle caps he had nailed pointed sides up to a piece of plywood. My mother and sister enjoyed knowing I was being controlled and punished. I am not sure my parents were aware of the other damages they caused. My location of punishment was always in front of a full-length mirror. There I knelt, my knees screaming out in pain with drips of blood evident from the puncture marks all the while staring into the big dark brown eyes of a little girl I learned to hate and despise. As tears rolled down the little girl's cheeks, inside me I felt nothing except hate for the weakness of the silent girl crying.

When I wasn't in enough trouble to suit my sister, she would instigate situations causing my parents to starve me, abuse me either physically or emotionally. I soon withdrew from life, love and from my family.

In my teenage years I discovered I was a product of my environment. I was moody, which my family doctor controlled with prescriptive tranquillizers, I drank constantly to numb the pain of life, but I could never out-run the loneliness.

One night in my late teens, I began drinking heavily. I began mixing my medication with the alcohol. It was at this moment I realized I reached a turning point and knew I had to end this existence. I got into my father's car and drove towards a majestic old maple tree outside of town. I believed smashing the car into that tree would end my pain. I despised my life, myself and everyone around me. As the wheels turned onto the gravel, the steering wheel was wrenched from my grip and I found myself back on the road. As I stopped the car, I felt a warm embrace envelope me and shower me with love. It was then I first heard the words, "You're not finished here yet." What had just happened? I was alone in the car! I didn't understand where the voice had come from. Later that night, I realized I had heard the voice of my Guardian Angel. This comforting voice I now recognize and have heard many times throughout my life.

I felt the presence of my Angel as I went through my own abusive and lonely marriage. Even though my Angel was mostly silent, each time I miscarried a pregnancy or asked, "Why?" or "Why did he break my nose again?" "Why can't anyone just love me." "Why did the only people I truly love (my maternal grandfather and paternal grandmother) have to die?" I realized I was not ready for the answers.

I endured a difficult marriage for twenty-five years. I was a wife, mother, elder care-giver, and abused woman who lost her identity, self-respect, and compassion, but always remained a student of human behavior. Throughout my life, my faith in God comforted and soothed me. The day I once again hit bottom, not knowing where to turn, I went to church to just be still. I sat staring at the face of Christ. My prayers must have been heard, for I know I witnessed a miracle. The face of Jesus appeared to turn and looked directly at me. I was washed with a love and warmth so pure and beautiful that I found the strength to go home and plan out my future. The only way for me to survive was to leave my marriage. It took me three years to accomplish this. During the divorce, I endured psychological abuse, such severe anxiety that I temporarily lost my eye-sight and was then faced with the death of my grandmother, the last person who loved me. Through it all I found courage and strength to keep moving forward. I knew I was here for a reason, but kept asking, "What is my purpose?"

Finally, free of my past life, I enrolled in college, and fell in love with a good friend. We were ready to build a life together based on mutual respect, understanding, love and friendship. Life was beginning to make sense.

In 2006, I graduated college, landed a great job, and in June of that year, Don and I were married. Life was great!

Eight months later, while trying to get home from work driving in a horrible ice and snow storm, I was hit head-on by a truck. Before the impact, I sat frozen in terror, believing I would die. With my hands locked in a death grip on the steering wheel, my right foot on the break, and jaw clenched, I waited and watched. I knew I was the intended target. In my terror, seconds before impact, I screamed out to God for help. Instantly, I calmed, felt the loving embrace and again heard the words, "You're not finished here yet."

I survived, but for the next ten years fought insurance companies, lawyers and the medical system. I was left with a brain injury, severe whiplash and a body filled with soft-tissue and spinal damage. Eventually I gave up. I was so beaten down and couldn't see my way through life. For ten years I lost my way, but began writing a book about my grandmother. I thought my purpose was to heal her soul. It was, but the plan was bigger than one person. By the time I finished my book, "A Century of Secrets," my soul had been freed of 57 years of pain, trauma, abuse and grief. The purpose for my book was to break the cycle of abuse, unlock the fear that keeps us prisoners and to show others that strength, courage, forgiveness and healing can be found.

This truth propelled me into coaching. I became a Certified Empowerment and Assertiveness Coach and launched my company, Sterling Silver Coaching. Through writing, exposing limiting beliefs and removing old programs from our pasts, we can heal, forgive, love and write our own futures. I continually study, observe and explore possibilities. Also, after experiencing the healing from NLP work, I enrolled in an NLP Certification Course. It is my goal to bring this important, life enhancing aspect to my clients.

It has taken a great deal of hardship, exploration, soul-searching and dedication to finally give voice to the gifts and abundance I have received. Proudly and with conviction I can honestly say, "I have accepted the gifts of compassion, healing, intuitiveness and love." I stand proud on my story and am sharing my gifts with the world. I now understand why, "I am not finished here yet." I dared to dream boldly and discovered my true path. I challenge you to be daring in your life and to dream boldly.

TERESA SYMS

Teresa Syms is an Award-Winning Author, Personal Empowerment and Assertiveness Coach. Born crippled into a dysfunctional and abusive family, Teresa has always been a fighter. Rising above her brutal childhood, an attempted suicide, an abusive marriage and near-death experience; all culminated into building a solid foundation for her passion as a coach and author. "You're not finished here yet" was whispered to her all her life. Teresa incorporates Neuro Linguistic Programming, assertiveness and unshakable faith with courage, to help others discover and realize, you're not finished here yet! Learn more at www.TeresaSyms.com or Teresa@SterlingSilverCoaching.com.

COLOR MY WORLD

BY ALLISON LINDGREN

Welcome dear friend to my country garden. It's my prayer you'll find comfort and healing here. I hope in talking together and in communing alone with God, you'll recover your relationship with your Heavenly Father.

What? You say you feel distanced from Him? When you try to seek Him, you believe the lies the enemy tells you that God couldn't love you the way you are; that you've used up all your second chances, that you're not good enough and there's no way he could ever use you. Then, you say the words that break my heart for you; as I too, have shared that same deep pain. "My life has become a series of epic failures," you say. "With every failure, I sink a little deeper into the pit of despair, and no matter how much I struggle, I can't seem to get out."

"I don't even see the color in the most beautiful areas of my life," you continue with tears brimming in your eyes. "My world has become a hazy grayscale, and I hate it! I can't believe God can use me when I wouldn't even choose me." These last words vehemently rush out of your mouth, and I reach out to wrap you in my arms and remind you that your Father God

176

already chose you. Even when you can't accept yourself, He loves you.

Sitting together on my porch, I pick up the china teapot, the one with the hand-painted blue roses and pour a cup of tea into the matching china cups. You watch the bright orange and black Monarch butterflies flit from one vibrant zinnia to another in the cacophony of color that lies below us, as you dab at your tears.

As you take a sip of your tea, I ask you if I can tell you my story; a story that began many years ago. For some reason, I believed that walking with God was protection from the terrible things that can happen in this world. Yes, I knew bad things happened to good people, but somehow, I thought I was different and that my faith could get me through anything. Except it didn't.

My story begins just after my much-older-than-average college graduation. When I dropped out of college at the age of 19, I always intended to return and one day earn my degree, but it didn't happen. When my long-time employer went out of business the same year our youngest daughter graduated from high school, I used that opportunity to deal with my empty nest, and I enrolled in college. That meant we had three people in college at the same time. My daughter and I graduated in the same ceremony, and my son was only six credits away. We had worked so hard, and I thought my life was great.

One day, knowing my summer vacation was soon going to be ending, a bright blue September sky beckoned me outdoors to enjoy those beautiful colors of fall. I laced up my sneakers, grabbed my camera and went in search of that elusive spectacular photo.

Capturing some great shots, I thoroughly enjoyed a long afternoon outdoors. I snapped pictures of the fall foliage; bright yellow cottonwood leaves that stretched into that deep blue sky, a great shot of a solitary leaf standing in sharp contrast against the gravel road it lay on, and pictures of a shiny, yellow, heart-shaped leaf held in place by dark green pine needles. The multi-shades of red and orange in the Ohio Buckeye tree was a diversion from the golds of the Cottonwoods and resulted in beautiful photos. I've always felt closest to God when I am in nature, and I remember thinking that day that life just couldn't get any better.

But two weeks later, it changed dramatically. A series of stressful life events hit us, one after another. We got knocked down, we got the wind knocked out of us, only to get up and get knocked down again and again. For this "pull yourself up by your bootstraps" kind of gal, it was difficult to accept that things were quickly spinning out of my control.

I'd always prided myself on being strong, and believed I

could make it through anything. Unfortunately, I failed miserably. Because I got angry with God for allowing all these things to hurt my family, I pulled away from Him and lost the strength, joy and comfort that I had grown to depend on.

The farther I got away from God, the uglier the self-talk in my head became; yet I still believed the lies. Most of us will admit that we have a mean voice inside our heads that criticizes us, often in a voice harsher than we'd ever use to talk to someone else. "You're such a failure." "You're so ugly." "You can't do anything right." "You're so fat." "I hate myself!" "I hate my life." Unfortunately, I started believing those words, words whose only purpose was to destroy what needed to be built up.

The rapid series of stressful life events, the negative self-talk I was only too willing to believe and turning my back on God, made my life miserable. I knew it needed to change. It took several years, but my first step was repentance. I asked God to lead my life and to guide me in what was now our "new normal." I then took the Social Readjustment Rating Scale, a measuring tool that gives life-changing events a different "weight" for stress-related events. The scores help us measure the load of stress we carry, and knowing the results help us make better stress-management decisions.

My score was extraordinarily high, and it told me I was at very high risk of becoming ill with a stress-related illness.

Illnesses like heart disease, asthma, obesity, diabetes, headaches, insomnia, depression and anxiety, gastrointestinal issues, Alzheimer's disease, and accelerated aging leading to premature death.

Stress isn't just a feeling, it's an actual physiologic response to a threat. When you're stressed, your body responds. Your blood vessels constrict, your pulse and blood pressure rise, and you breathe faster. Hormones, like cortisol and adrenaline, flood your bloodstream. During long-term stress, these physiologic changes can lead to health problems. However, studies show that stress management techniques not only make you feel better, they also have real health benefits like decreasing the risk of a second heart attack and improving immunity. Although we'll never be able to remove all stress from our lives, we can change how we respond to it. Stress management is just a matter of learning to take care of you, and it's why self-care is so important.

Christians, especially women, feel guilty for taking care of themselves. We've been taught to put others ahead of ourselves, but sometimes, it's necessary to put ourselves first so we can be emotionally healthy again. God cares about all aspects of our health, emotional and physical.

The following activities from my forthcoming book (scheduled for December 2017 release) titled "Take Care of You;

A 30 Day Journey to a More Positive You," are only part of your daily journey, as you work with God to become a more positive you; reducing stress, negativity and opening your eyes to the good that is all around us! If God can take my hazy, grayscale life and transform it into vibrant hues in full living color, I know He can do it for you, too.

Excerpt from Take Care of You: A 30 Day Journey to a More Positive You:

1. Set aside quiet time to talk to God. Jesus regularly felt the need to get away from people and spend time alone with God in prayer. Sometimes, we just need to make the decision that we want to hear God speak and ask Him to do so. A powerful exercise in the book heightens your ability to listen as God speaks to you.

2. Focus on the moment. Are you living in the present? Or are you living in the future or the past? If you're worried about what to do next or regretful about something you've already done; confess it to God, forgive yourself and move on. That's what grace is for.

3. Be kind to yourself. Remember, God loves you and doesn't say things to you that aren't beneficial to you. When harmful thoughts surface in your mind, remember those thoughts are not coming from God. Think about what is true, and focus on what's right. Use this time to dream boldly, and discern which dreams are the God-sized dreams God has planned for you.

4. Keep your problems in perspective. While it seems too simple, the next time you're feeling stressed, think about the things for which you're grateful. Even in bad times, I can still remind myself that I'm lucky in the most basic ways. I have a loving family, a roof over my head, and I can once again see the beauty of the world around me in all its vivid colors.

ALLISON LINDGREN

Allison Lindgren is an award-winning journalist and columnist. She specializes in human interest stories; softer stories that tend to humanize the news. Her weekly column, Eyes That See the Good in Things, has the same goal. As a transformational author, her forthcoming book, "Take Care of You: A 30-Day Challenge for a More Positive You," is scheduled for release in December, 2017. She is fiercely committed to helping people work through stressful life events, as they're guided toward a more positive response. Learn more at AllisonLindgren.com.

WHAT STORY ARE YOU LIVING?

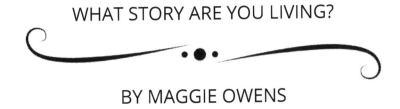

BY MAGGIE OWENS

We either own our story or our story owns us. If we own our story, we get to write the ending. If our story owns us, we'll relive it again and again until we learn the lesson.

I've discovered my life is determined less by past events than by the way I remember them. It's taken years to uncover the real me, and to separate myself from the things that happened to me.

I am reminded of a Native American parable about a grandfather who says, "I feel as if I have two wolves fighting in my heart. One wolf is the vengeful, angry one. The other wolf is the loving, compassionate one." When asked, which wolf will win the fight in his heart, the old man replied. "The one I feed."

I began to observe the version of events I "feed" my heart. At times, I remembered and shared stories with myself and others that were strengthening and healing; but more often, the stories darkened as I relived my past, thereby remaining stuck in the very pain that brought me here. This variability was draining, and the highs and lows kept me perpetually unsettled. Negative patterns continued to repeat themselves. Another abuser, more manipulation, taken advantage of again. Each night my creative imagination took the worst of it and invented even greater deception. I didn't realize then that my subconscious mind would manifest all my greatest fears in my day to day life.

I am a survivor of sexual abuse and domestic violence. I can say with absolute certainty that I did not know what love was, until I knew what it was not. From all outward appearances, I had it all. By any standard, I would have been considered successful. I made persistent efforts to do the right thing, lived from a kind heart, achieved tops marks in my graduate program, and worked hard in an executive level career for companies reputed to be the best. However, once I committed to any situation – whether a relationship or a cross-country move for a new position – the life I carefully constructed would implode. I experienced every conceivable form of betrayal, duplicity, and treachery. That sweet guy courting me was really a closet alcoholic; the person publicly recognized for outstanding service was soon exposed for fraud in his non-profit executive position; the leader of the church was a bigamist. Without searching for the bad, it seemed drawn to me. At every turn, I encountered unscrupulous behaviors and malfeasance.

I survived, because of my absolute faith that God was my

protector and redeemer, but my journey back to myself began while single parenting my daughter Julia. Her very existence compelled me toward healing. I wanted for her what I couldn't accept for myself, and that became my driving motivation. I foolishly assumed my own brokenness did not matter, and I told myself no one could hurt me any more than I had already been hurt. Through the years, I gave up expecting anything good for myself, and instead, put all my thoughts and efforts into creating and supporting my daughter's life, while living vicariously through her. While I continued to experience the ups and downs of a survivor in recovery, I buried the impact. I stopped trying to understand or change the cycle of abuse, and instead worked hard to be a good mother, praying the dark side was invisible to my daughter.

Julia was laughter, love and light, and I was mesmerized by her joyous living and whole-hearted loving. My child was an extreme extrovert being raised by an extreme introvert. Her idea of relaxing was having twenty of her best friends come over, so our house became the place to hang. Her happiness became my happiness; her laughter became music to my ears. With a strong sense of right and wrong, and an even stronger work ethic, Julia responded best to parenting by the Socratic method. In turn, I re-captured many of my 'lost years.' Julia graduated college in three and a half years with double majors in Theatre and Communication. Yes, she always wanted to be an actor and singer and her favorite color is still rainbow!

After college graduation, my daughter moved to the Twin Cities and worked for the Minneapolis Musical Theatre and the Children's Theatre Company while teaching at the St Paul Music Academy. Two years later, she had her first "solo" apartment on the Mississippi River, and soon thereafter, took a much-needed break to go on a Boundary Waters Canoe trip in Northern Minnesota. It was a difficult journey for four women. Portaging the canoes and carrying all their supplies was heavy work, but oh, so beautiful, in the million-acre sanctuary. They call it 'God's Country' and market to women and church youth groups.

On their last night, six men came into their campground. Three of them lured her friends away and three drugged her and dragged her a quarter mile into the woods and gang raped her. When her friends began looking for her, the men dragged her further into the brush and continued. When the girls finally wandered to her vicinity in the pitch-dark forest, one man ran away, one man ran forward to stall them, and the third man held a gun to her back telling her to say she is 'fucking fine' or they will rape them or kill them all. Julia said she was fine. "I'm fine. I'm fine. I'm fine. I'm fine." She heard the guys laugh and high five one another for the "three-way" while canoeing away. One man came back into her tent and tried to rape her again, leaving

10 bullets near her head as a reminder.

Julia did not tell the girls that night. She threw up repeatedly and cried and shook. She hoped for morning. There are no forester patrols and no call boxes in the million-acre woods. Dawn came. The girls paddled an entire day to safety. When they made it to shore, Julia told them what happened. Her friend from college teased her saying she was just drunk and fooling around in the woods and now she's feeling guilty. On their drive back to the Twin Cities, she texted me she was fine; her phone was dying, and she could not talk. Her friends laughed and joked all the way home. No hospital. No police. Julia texted her best friend the whole story as the flashbacks rolled over her. Back in the Cities her "friends" told her to unpack. They said she was slow. They called her "dramatic." They dropped her off and left. She spent the night in the fetal position and showered in her clothes. She then drove to South Dakota. "Mom, I'm home."

Ultimately, these savage men were found, but only three of the six were interviewed, one of the three via voice message. The Minnesota Bureau of Criminal Apprehension said to one of the perpetrators, "If you tell us it was he said, she said, we have to believe you." We have the case files and transcripts. We have all their names and addresses. The County Prosecutor denied a crime victim's advocate. He told Julia if she testified, it would likely be construed as "partying that got out of control." There were no search warrants or arrests. The legal system stalled and finally, denied prosecution.

Darkness descends like a shroud, snuffing out my breath. Impending doom! I cloak myself in dung; yes, I am familiar with this scent. The watcher in me waits and wonders, will we rise again?

> *Darkness descends like a shroud, sniffing out my breath. Impending doom! I cloak myself; yes, I am familiar with this scent. The watcher in me waits and wonders will we rise again?*

The crime had been so carefully planned and executed, it seemed likely this was not their first time. CBS Affiliate station WCCO (Liz Collin, Minneapolis), aired a 10:33 minute news segment covering Julia's case, thereby raising awareness and concern for safety precautions in the Boundary Waters and prosecutorial integrity. Two years later, we were not surprised when the County Prosecutor was convicted and jailed for two counts of criminal sexual misconduct. He was fired soon thereafter, and the Minnesota Supreme Court has indefinitely suspended his license. Julia's case was used as a training exercise for the Sexual Violence Justice Institute and the Minnesota Coalition Against Sexual Assault to improve the justice system and crime victim advocacy. The six perpetrators, older men who had been friends since childhood, still live in the Twin Cities. It's likely they party at the same camp site in the Boundary Waters for a week each year, as they had for many years prior.

My daughter's brutal sexual assault happened six years ago. While I was strong when caring for her, sifting through the excruciating details of the case, and sorting through the corruption, the deepening chasm of despair became a sink hole pulling me under, and I came close to suicide. By default, my identity and salvation came through her. My only worth in life came from keeping my daughter safe and insuring her life was better than mine. But often, survivors don't initially need or want your help; in fact, they may even push those closest to them away. I was reeling, and my world was spinning.

I realize now, I had given up on myself decades prior. I accepted, even embraced, my identity as the traumatized victim of circumstances too painful to recover from. But that worked only as long as my daughter was fine, and life was nowhere close to that. During this period, I was foster mother to a sexually abused two-year-old girl with a reactive attachment diagnosis, and my daughter was struggling through post-traumatic stress disorder. My insurance was inadequate to cover her needs, so I closed my business and left teaching to go back into the corporate-world, a business arena I previously found to be painful and punishing, Chaos was the only thing that felt normal to me.

You cannot escape a prison if you don't know you're in one. Slowly it dawned on me that at my funeral, the saddest thing would not be the death of my body (that would be a mere formality), it would be the death of all my unfulfilled dreams and aspirations. It's that trip I was going to take and never took. The business I was going to start and never started. The book I was going to write and never wrote. The love I was meant to have and never experienced. I kept myself so frantically 'busy,' there was no time to feel anything other than the past. I blocked or sabotaged all new relationships, jobs, and experiences. I became a highly sensitive person prone to emotional outbursts, suspecting everyone of ulterior motives and innuendo. Outside of work, I isolated myself. I even met with a psychiatrist to consider getting a lobotomy. It seemed easier to continue to sabotage myself than to move forward and build a life, but I refused to go to the grave with my music still inside of me.

Heaven is a state of mind. I have learned that my mind, my very own thoughts, were a primary source and cause of the conditions in my life. Our thinking power flows in us and through us like the very air we breathe. I began to examine the things that dominated my daily thinking. Was I controlling my thoughts or were my thoughts controlling me? Who was this helpless victim to whom bad things kept happening? I learned that what my mind holds within, takes form in my outer world. Giving into worries, fears and negativity had continually broken down my mental state, leaving me vulnerable and despairing. When my thoughts were misdirected, unfocused and uncontrolled, I created even more pain and confusion. My goal then, was to channel my powers constructively and to begin using my thinking capacity for 'good.'

A person harvests whatever is planted. If you want corn, but you plant carrot seeds, you will never get corn. Powerlessness is the most dangerous state one can experience. It is rooted with shame and watered by self-fulfilled prophecies. If I really attract what I believe about myself, then I had to learn to control my thoughts. I felt both of our lives depended upon it. I could no longer fake it; I needed true transformation. The stakes were too high. I must become the greatest version of myself, which meant figuring out my self-worth, my calling, my deepest aspirations, and learning to live from my higher side. When I changed my thinking, I changed my life.

Today, I remain intentionally grounded in my own life. As a result, my relationships and experiences have dramatically improved. I've calmed my internal dialogue and re-framed my self-limiting beliefs from negativity and scarcity, to hope, trust, and abundance. When filled with pain, I seek comfort and joy. When darkness immerses me, I remember my future aspirations, and feel it as if I am living it right now. I realize that fear can only live within me when I put my energy into it, and I refuse to feed fear. After all, both fear and faith ask us to believe in something we cannot see. I choose faith!

Experience is no teacher unless I learn from it. I now understand that life is not what happens to me, it is what happens in me and through me because of the experience. I choose to live from the inside out, in an outside in world, and to be redeemed by the very acts that harmed me.

Today, Julia is happily married and loves to cuddle with her newborn son. She completed her Master of Education in Theatre, Communication, and English, and serves as Theatre Director and Teacher at her local high school. Maggie and Julia share their stories through books, articles and speaking engagements to offer hope, encouragement, and strategies for cope with crisis and responding with resilience. You can participate in these important conversations through Maggie and Julia's "There's No Shame" initiative. Join the conversation at http://theresnoshame.com where you will find a community in which to speak out, advocate and experience recovery.

MAGGIE OWENS

Maggie owns Human Capital Consultants, and co-owns Ethic Consulting, and Athena Rise (a leadership development and entrepreneurship group run by women for women). She approaches work and life with a people-first philosophy, helping individuals and groups change habits and shift paradigms using Thinking into Results and other personal and organizational development assessments and tools. Maggie continues to advocate for and support survivors of trauma. If you are ready to improve your personal or professional life and want to transform your results, Maggie invites you to connect with her at maggie@humancc.biz.

I AM FREE

BY CLARISSA VANN

Dear Clarissa,

For years, you have carried the shame from believing that you allowed your innocence to be taken. You carried resentment toward your body for developing so full, so young, and drawing in the attention of men. You have spent years being committed to blaming and punishing yourself for being naïve. You believed for so long that because your body responded with orgasm, you must have wanted it. He never had the right to touch your 12, 13, 14, 15, 16 or 17-year-old body. You have worn the burden of your past for so long, but now, my child, it is time for you to release the experience and make peace.

For years you said "No." You really believed in your heart, when he said he loved you like you were his own child, that he'd never hurt you. You learned very early on, that people say things they don't mean, and break promises they never intended to honor. You didn't understand that his intentions weren't pure.

First, uncomfortable touches in the most sacred places, while others in the house were sleeping, and soon it would turn into more. You believed him when he said he simply couldn't

195

control himself. You even believed him when he said you wanted him. You've carried this shame like an old worn-out backpack, but it's time to release it.

When you finally gained the strength and courage to tell, the ones called to protect you didn't listen. You felt unprotected, unloved, and all alone. When you finally gained the courage to share your story with the man you loved the most, he didn't believe you, and later used it against you to hurt you.

Despite all the pain Clarissa, there is a miracle that awaits you. Your experience will silently help you change the lives of thousands of women. Your pain will become your purpose, and you will find that your lesson becomes your powerful message. There is no shame. You are not to blame. You are healed. You are whole. You are free!

CLARISSA VANN

Clarissa Vann is a mom of four, and a holistic health coach that's passionate in teaching people how to listen to their body with tips and knowledge to lead them to ultimate health. She also owns a successful network marketing business with Pruvit International, where she educates people on the healing power of exogenous ketones. Connect with Clarissa via email at clarissavannhhc@gmail.com or via Facebook @ facebook.com/prbyclarissa

YOUR STORY ISN'T OVER

BY STEPHANIE KVIDERA

On June 23rd, 1980, I became a big sister. I was four years old and proud to be a big sister to Stacy Lynn. Fast forward to Saturday morning, August 30th, 2014; this was the day my family's life would change forever. The word suicide would now be part of our story. Stacy had taken her own life, and she took her cat with her.

She was my only sibling. As a young child, she was always coloring, drawing and loved animals. Of course, we fought like all siblings do, but as adults we grew closer. She was beautiful; one of the smartest people in school, and had tons of friends. Everyone loved her.

We were born and raised in NW Iowa. She moved to Alabama in 2004 when she accepted a job as the veterinary technician at the Montgomery zoo. God gave her a special gift when it came to caring for animals. From the time she was a child, all she ever wanted to do was take care of animals. I had the privilege of seeing first-hand how truly special her gift really was in working with her zoo animals. She loved them all and it was clear they loved her back (especially the chimps)!

From the outside looking in she seemed to have it all; her dream job, her own home, a dog, a cat, and a bearded dragon. She seemed to finally be in a good place, and the happiest I had seen her in a very long time during my last visit to see her in October 2013. Her eyes lit up when she talked about the man she was dating and they were planning a future together. Little did I know at the time, this man (that I did not meet for the first time until her funeral service in Montgomery) and I would become instrumental to one another's healing process, but most importantly, he became my only brother. To this day, he still calls me his sister and I'm eternally grateful for him in my life.

Those who knew Stacy well, knew about her struggles with depression, the anxiety, and the daily pain she was in from an invisible illness called Fibromyalgia. No matter what she endured though, she was always there for her friends when they needed someone to talk to. She cared so deeply for everyone and everything, that she made their problems and worries her own. She was doing all the things she was supposed to, for her physical and mental health. She regularly went to her doctor's appointments and took her prescribed medications. The varieties of meds she took didn't always mix well and would cause her depression to spiral out of control sometimes. I strongly believe this caused the demons in her head to ultimately win the battle against her in the end. We've been told that those who commit suicide often don't want to die. They're often the most sensitive, and commit the act to end the pain and suffering to find peace.

The morning of August 30th my parents called. I remember the instant feeling of dread placed in the pit of my stomach. Somehow, I knew it was about my sister, but no one could have prepared me for the words my dad said. "Stacy's dead. She killed herself." I couldn't think straight, and I remember yelling at my parents telling them it wasn't true. How could they say something like that? She wouldn't do that to herself! I repeated that over and over and in a panic, I dropped the phone on the living room floor. In a state of shock, I spent the three-hour drive home looking out the window from the passenger seat. I didn't speak a single word the whole way. It wasn't until we got to my parents house that I found out exactly how she did it. She purchased a gun at a pawn shop a couple of days before. She had the whole thing planned out, right down to the smallest details according to the pages of handwritten notes she left behind. It was the scariest thing I've ever read. She was at peace with her decision. To her it made perfect sense, but to us it was like pieces of a puzzle that we will never be able to put together because of what's missing. The one thing she kept repeating across every page was that she needed peace.

Peace became a theme with her funeral services. We held two services for her; one in Alabama, and the other in our hometown, where she was laid to rest. This heart wrenching process was the longest two weeks of our lives. Our entire family was physically, mentally and emotionally drained to say the least.

On the flight home following her funeral, I flew by myself. This was my first time flying alone, and only my third time ever flying. I was scared, but I did it without getting lost, and I was proud of myself for having the strength to fly alone during one of the most painful experiences ever. I printed my boarding pass and it said I didn't have a seat number. The flight was overbooked. I would have to wait for another plane, along with several others that were supposed to be on the same flight. Emotionally, I was a wreck. I was feeling all alone, and all I wanted was to get home. I sat in a "fog" for a while and then a miracle occurred. My name was announced over the loud speaker and they were able to get me on the plane after all. I was so relieved and even got a second-row seat! Once seated, I leaned my head against the window and started processing all the events that had taken place over the past couple of days. Silent tears flowed down my face. A man sat next to me. After a bit, he asked me where I was headed. I told him I was going home to Iowa. He asked if I had fun in Alabama. I told him I was there for my sister's funeral. His whole demeanor changed and his face became somber. He shared that he was a minister at one of the Baptist churches in Montgomery. From out of his bag, he pulled out his worn bible and asked if he could pray with me. The entire rest of the flight home, he read me bible verses and talked about God. He was the angel I needed in that very moment, when I thought I wasn't getting a seat on that overbooked plane. I truly believe in my heart that God and Stacy had a plan all along to put the two of us together on that plane, in those seats next to each other, to give me peace and comfort on my way home.

A year after Stacy's death was our parents 40th wedding anniversary. I went shopping by myself to pick out a special gift. I was having an incredibly hard time with it because Stacy was supposed to be helping me. I needed her input in making decisions. While in the store, I sat in tears torn between two different gifts. To my surprise, I heard Stacy's voice tell me which one to pick. It was so clear! So, I chose that frame and had it engraved. Later that night, I had the most incredible dream that I'll never forget. I was holding a double 8x10 photo frame up to my face, one like our mom used to put our school pictures in and display on top of the console tv. Suddenly, someone grabbed my arms. This person put a hand on top of the photo frame and pushed it down, so I could see her face. I gasped and said, "oh my God, you look just like my sister!" She said, "it's me, Steph, it's really me!" I started sobbing uncontrollably. She hugged me as real as any hug I've ever had in my life and in my left ear she whispered, "I still think about what I did and I'm so sorry." Then just like that, she was gone. I began looking around the room I was in and realized I was standing in the living room of the childhood home we grew up in. It was decorated the same as I remember it.

Suicide grief is unlike any other kind of grief. I've learned that grief is different for each person and nobody grieves in the same way. There is no right or wrong way. I don't think one ever stops the grieving process once we're forced to embrace it. It's a personal journey and individual to each person. It ebbs and flows, changing from day to day.

For the past three years, I've participated in the Out of the Darkness Community Walk here in central Iowa, hosted by the American Foundation of Suicide Prevention (afsp.org). The first year I went, I was astounded at the number of people walking for loved ones they had lost to suicide. Roughly 1000 people attended. It's saddening, but at the same time I finally knew I wasn't alone. There's a very supportive community full of folks to help with the grief and healing process. According to the afsp.org's website, suicide is the 10th leading cause of death in the United States. Suicide awareness has now become a personal mission of mine. I realize that it makes some people uncomfortable to talk about, but that shouldn't be the case. Educate yourself. Be the voice for those fighting the fight, and for those who gave up the fight. I vow to keep my little sister's legacy alive, for as long as I have breath in my body. Your story isn't over. My story continues...

If you or someone you know feels suicidal, please call the National Suicide Prevention Lifeline for help: 1-800-273-8255, or text 741741 for free and confidential support for any crisis if you prefer not to talk. Please don't become another statistic. Suicide doesn't have to be the answer.

STEPHANIE KVIDERA

Stephanie Kvidera is a wife and mom of two teenage sons, two dogs and a tortoise. She is a full-time graphic artist with 21 years of experience. She works for the largest magazine fulfillment company in the country as an art and production specialist; preparing magazine publishers direct mail, bills and renewals for print. In her spare time, she enjoys watching her boys play baseball, football, and run track. She also owns a home-based business selling personalized, storytelling keepsake jewelry. Connect @ www.facebook.com/stephanie.kvidera.

FOR THE LOVE OF 31

BY BRANDIE MITCHELL

Let me begin by stating how honored I am to be part of this project. Our world is in tremendous need of positivity, acts of kindness, inspiration, and motivation. I'm hoping this story can be one small way for me to contribute.

My life has been a full and happy one, for many reasons, but largely due to the two people I'm about to share with you. A few weeks before my fifth birthday, a special angel was brought into my life. My sister, Tamara Lee (Tammy), was born. She was beautiful in every way and I simply adored her. She had made me a big sister and I felt like I was on top of the world. Due to some very unfortunate circumstances, her physical abilities were taken away when she was a few months old. She was unable to walk, talk, feed herself, use the restroom, and many other tasks we often take for granted. This began my family's new journey, with changing roles and lots of learning. Without going into depth, Tammy had many trials and tribulations over the years, which meant her loved ones did too; but her happiness, achievements, and love overcame any adversity. She loved country music (Randy Travis in particular), going to the ballpark, being with her friends at school (especially the naughty ones), eating pizza, and being silly with her family. I swear that she understood much more than she was able to tell us. I'm not going to lie; sometimes I was thankful she couldn't talk, because she was the keeper of all my secrets. That girl's eyes told everything you needed to know. Her smile could literally light up the room, and when she achieved a milestone, we all got to celebrate her.

After 29 short years, the Lord decided Tammy's room was ready. As my grandma would say, she went to be with Him, to watch over all of us. This was an extremely difficult time for my family and I, especially my mom, as she had been Tammy's "primary caregiver" for all her years with us. Those two words don't seem nearly significant enough for all Mom did, for all the love she gave Tammy and our family. Once again roles changed, and we endured lots of new beginnings.

On what would have been Tammy's 30th birthday, several of us came together and released 30 multi-colored balloons. Just as we were finishing, it began to sleet. The weather change was totally unexpected, so we all ran to our cars. Once we were safely inside, we turned back to look at where we'd been standing just a few moments earlier. The sleet quickly stopped and right before our eyes was the most beautiful rainbow we've ever seen. It was so bright, vibrant, and seemed to be full of life, just as our Tammy had been. We were there to celebrate her birthday, but what a wonderful gift she gave to us, in that healing moment, when we knew she received our message and that she was ok.

That's how it always was with Tammy; I often felt like I was giving so much of myself to her, but in the end, she had given me so much more. She was the ultimate "teacher" and as I was going through college to become one, I always said that she taught me way more than any textbook or class could have done. She taught me to have empathy (not sympathy), how to care for others, determination, selflessness, and acceptance. Most importantly, she taught me about the purest form of love, the kind of love you have when you tell your sister a secret and her eyes tell you "I understand, and your secret's safe with me." This is the kind of love you feel when your little sister is nervous and upset, and you finally feel her fingers relax around yours after singing her favorite song. As if that's not enough, she also gave me many things that impact my life to this day. She gave me confidence, knowledge, understanding, and experience. She gave me the opportunity to work at the summer school she attended and meet many other special people. People who have become family. People who understand me, and the rest of my family because they've experienced some of the same things. That job, and those people, have led to other opportunities which include having my own classroom now. Tamara Lee was the first person who set that ball in motion and I would have never achieved it without her, and the knowledge I gained because of her life. I am forever grateful and can only wish that my life will have as much meaning as hers did.

Another special person in my life was my grandpa. I say "was" because he was also called Home just a few months ago. Although I take comfort in knowing he and Tamara, and many other loved loves, are together now, this world just isn't the same without them.

When anyone talks about my grandpa, Fred Stolen, baseball always enters the conversation at some point. Although he was involved in every part of my life, our relationship was ingrained at the ballpark, where we spent most of our summers together. You see, Grandpa was a baseball legend around Sioux City, IA as it had been a part of his life since he was a young boy. Between playing, umping, and coaching, he had been in baseball for 50 years by the time I turned sixteen. He was drafted by what was then the New York Giants baseball team to be a pitcher and/or third baseman. At that time, professional baseball players didn't make much money and he had just married my grandma, so Grandpa turned down the offer. I often teased him about the possibility of him owning an MLB team now had he taken the offer, but deep down I was always happy he hadn't gone. If he had, I probably wouldn't have gotten to spend so much time with him, nor had the baseball experiences I encountered over the years. He decided to put his passion for baseball to use in other ways.

Not only did he coach several family members over the years, he also served as a pitching coach at different times, at both local colleges, Morningside and Briar Cliff, and started his own semi-pro team, the Sioux City Saints. He happened to start up the team the same summer I was born, in 1975. I've always thought that was meant to be! He coached the team, cared for the field, and grew the love of baseball in our city for 21 years. Everyone who had anything to do with baseball around here, always recognized #31 and his bright orange Saints hat.

From the time I was a little girl, I remember going to the ballpark with Grandpa. He always asked if I wanted to go help him with the field, get the concession stand ready, run to Hauff's Sporting Goods for equipment, or head to a game. I became the team's batgirl, which was one of the highlights of my life. Grandpa, and all the players, made me feel like I was part of the team; like I belonged, which hadn't happened a lot at that point in my life. I came to embrace the same passion for baseball that Grandpa had. That time spent, and love of the game shared, are just two of the many gifts he gave me.

As Grandpa grew older, and his eyes got worse, he had

to give up coaching, but his love for the game never died. We often had debriefings over the phone about a game on TV or went to watch someone play. He got to help "coach" my son, Josh, over the years, and watching them practice together was one of the greatest joys in my life. Another gift he gave to me.

One time when Grandpa was in the hospital, I was just beginning my new job (at the time) as a sign language interpreter in the schools. I was extremely overwhelmed trying to learn all the signs needed to support my students and help them be successful. Mind you, Grandpa was laying in the hospital bed, not well at all, but he was the one supporting me. I remember him taking my hand and telling me to relax and just take it one day at a time, that I didn't have to learn everything in one day, and that he knew I could do it. A few years later when I went back to college to get my teaching degree, I was overwhelmed once again and scared to death. Again, he reassured me that I was doing the right thing and that I could do it. More gifts he gave to me! His belief in me allowed me to believe in myself, and encouragement to go after my dreams, no matter how hard they may be.

Now, as with all of us, this earth was only his temporary home. His last few days here with us, were probably the hardest of my life. I tried to do what he did for me; I held his hand, gave him reassurance that everything would be ok, sang him songs (including Take Me Out to the Ballgame of course), and was simply just there.

When my sister left this earth, I always looked for signs. I needed to know she was ok and maybe that she was still nearby. She's given me a few over the years, but not nearly as many as she gave my niece. They were very close and Tammy dying was the first loss my young niece had had to deal with in her life. Maybe my niece needed those signs more than me.

When Grandpa died, I wondered what would happen. Well, let me tell you. I always know my grandpa is always around, especially when I need some reassurance. The number 31 shows up all over the place and I know it's him saying "hello!" Recently, I was talking to my friend about Grandpa and how much I missed him. When we hung up the phone, I looked at my screen. The time was 7:31 and it was 31 degrees outside. His number has shown up on how many notifications or emails I have, a dollar amount at the store, the only number not covered on one of my student's Bingo card, the winning score in a 9-hole round of golf at a golf tournament in honor of him, and so many other places. I thank God for the peaceful moments and Grandpa for the signs. I've come to believe that those signs are given to the one who needs it, at the exact time we need it most.

In conclusion, I'm beyond grateful for these two people, gifted to me, and to those who have impacted my life positively.

I've found it immensely important to surround yourself with good people. Truly listen them. Open your eyes, and your heart, and take it all in. Use all your knowledge, not only what can be gained from a textbook. Go after your dreams and don't let anything stop you. Things may not always turn out the way you think they will; in the end, they usually turn out better!

Allow your heart to guide you forward, and when you need a sign, simply ask and it will be revealed to you. Get quiet, listen closely and watch for the miracles in disguise.

BRANDIE MITCHELL

Brandie answers to Mom, Brandie Lynn, Babe, Sissy, Mrs. Mitchell, Batgirl, B, or several others that may not be appropriate for this enclosure. She's been a respite care provider for 26 years and a first-grade teacher for over 8 years. She's been married to her soul mate for 22 years, and together they have a 19-year-old son, Joshua. She feels blessed by holding so many roles throughout her life, but these are her most significant, by far.

UNCONDITIONAL LOVE

BY JULIE NELSEN

Ever since I was a little girl growing up on a farm in rural Nebraska, I have always felt my life was blessed beyond anything that I could even understand. I have always had the feeling of joy and thankfulness in my heart, and have always been blessed beyond my wants or needs. Was life perfect for me? No, as a matter of fact. There have been times it's been extremely difficult, but my faith and love of God was embedded in me before I can even remember, and always got me through. The funny thing is, I never really knew what I had until later in life.

One of my earliest memories was when I was two-years-old. My mom and dad were getting married. I remember my mom getting ready, and she was standing in the window with her wedding dress on. My dad stood at the alter waiting for her, and I sat in the church pew wanting to be up there with them. I finally had a family! (My mom was later surprised I remembered all the details).

When I was around six-years-old, I was sitting in a chair watching my mom work around the kitchen. It was there that I first learned I was adopted by my dad. The way my mom

215

explained it to me actually made me feel very special. She told me how my adopted dad chose both of us, and how his parents loved me from the beginning. I was Grandpa's little girl, and followed him everywhere on the farm. I felt like the luckiest girl to be loved so much, by so many, and actually went to school bragging about how I was adopted!

A few years later, I began to question why "Mike" didn't love me. Instead of feeling bad, I began to dislike him very much. I would tell myself that a guy who chose alcohol over his daughter was not nice, and I would dismiss his title even as my "biological father." I wanted no part of him being my dad, yet quietly wondered about him and why he let me go.

Across my teens, 20's and most of my 30's, I hid my fears of never being good enough for my dad. After I was married, I wondered if I was good enough for my husband, and often questioned if he'd stop loving me too. I felt like I'd never be enough.

It wasn't until I stood in my church office talking to a friend about her addictions, that I began to understand the illness of what "Mike" had. I experienced a sense of relief, but still it was hard to accept. I threw myself into loving my own family, and found more joy than anything being a wife and mother. With all that I had within me, I loved everyone I possibly could, which always came easy for me. It's so important to me that people feel loved. Matthew 22:37-39 says "Gods greatest commandment is to Love God with all your heart and all your soul, to love his people and to love your neighbor as yourself." This was easy for me.

As my kids grew, my role as a parent changed. This left me with a lot of time, and I didn't know what to do. I didn't have any direction as to where I was going, I didn't know how to act, and my insecurities of not being loved or feeling good enough, were starting to haunt me again. I didn't know who I was or what I wanted to do, so I looked to my husband to keep me happy, as I was living in a fear I couldn't really understand.

While we should have been celebrating, my insecurities got the best of me, and on the 25th year of our marriage, we were divorced. Now I was on my own to figure out who I was and where I was going. I was so down on myself, I didn't want to be around anyone. I lived life the way I thought I'd wanted, grabbing onto anything that felt good in the moment, but I was spiraling down quickly. I would pray almost every night "Lord, please don't let me go." Do you want to know what? He didn't!

Over these past five years, I have learned a lot about myself. While things haven't always turned out the way I think they should, I have been given grace, and He has shown me *unconditional love*. I have so much more I want to be, do and see. My favorite verse (and I believe it with my whole heart) is James

1:2-4. It tells us to be joyful in all trials and tribulations, because in our trying times, we have an opportunity to grow so much, we have a God who will see us through it and we become closer to Him. I myself, choose to be defined by God!

Over the years, I have known He can pull me through my mistakes, my heart aches, and all the mishaps that happen in my lifetime. I am so fortunate to have an amazing family with a strong support system, and we love one another through all the ups & downs of life. God places certain people or events in our paths, and it's our choice as to how we'll unwrap the gifts and recognize what's been placed before us.

I want to share a reminder to cherish your loved ones. Our family has lost some very close family members that really took a toll on me. At the age of nineteen, my brother died suddenly. I loved him so much and never got to tell him how he affected my life. He truly was placed in our family for a purpose and I believe (beyond a doubt) God planned it. This past February, my ex-father-in-law passed away. I am so grateful I was able to tell him how much I loved him, and shared how much I'd miss him. I was able to tell him what he meant to me, and how important his life was to me. That man was an amazing man, and a great role model for our family. Talk about love! His heart was huge, and he taught us all so much about how to love one another.

A few months ago, I lost my beautiful mother to lung cancer via a stroke caused by the side effects of her cancer treatments. The woman who protected her little girl from any harm as best as she could, and sheltered me from the ugliness of alcoholism, was gone. She left us all too quickly, yet as we were going through it, the pain felt like an eternity. At her funeral, friends shared what she'd endured for my sisters and I, and we were amazed! We had no idea! There was a lot we never understood until she was on her death bed. She was the one to introduce me to God, and the reason I have a solid foundation in my faith. She taught my sisters and I that when we don't understand something, to be a little more patient. Pray and trust that there's is reason. And she was right!

This past September of 2017, my daughter (Brylie), got married. While this was supposed to be the happiest moment of her life, it was difficult. She had lost her grandfather (who meant the world to her), followed by my mom (her grandma), who she was incredibly close to. My mom was so excited for Brylie's wedding day! She'd ask Brylie questions and couldn't wait to see her dress. So, when the big day came and neither of them were with us to celebrate, there was a lot of sadness. It was a gloomy day and it had been raining off and on. The wedding was set to be held outside, and we even contemplated holding it inside because of the weather, but decided to keep it outdoors and hope for the best.

The wedding procession began, and the skies got really dark. The moment Brylie stepped outside with her father, the clouds parted, and it was as if God opened the sky up; as the sun shined brightly upon all of us, keeping us all so warm. In the distance, we could all see the gloomy, dark skies, but there was only sunlight as my daughter walked down the aisle. When the pastor began speaking, some misty raindrops fell like tears falling from heaven, but it was strange because none of us really got wet. All of a sudden, a vibrant rainbow appeared, shining so brightly over the entire ceremony and encompassing our friends and family. Within minutes, another rainbow appeared. What a blessing! The moment the ceremony was complete, the rainbows quietly disappeared. What a gift for God to open up the sky and give Brylie's grandparents the best seats in the house! Everyone felt the love, and it truly was a miracle sent from heaven with love.

Beyond any doubt, the joy I hold in my heart is from a God who loved me first, a mother who protected me as best as she could, a father who "chose" me, sisters whom I have an incredible bond, a brother whom I loved so much, so many amazing friends that I can't even begin to describe ,and my children. They are my greatest blessings. Thank you Lord, for never letting me go!

I would like to end in sharing a few of my favorite verses with you. When I said, "My foot is slipping," your unfailing love Lord, supported me. When anxiety was great within me, your consolation brought me joy." (Psalm 94:17-18)

"Consider it pure joy, my brothers and sisters, whenever you face trials of many kinds, because you know that the testing of your faith produces perseverance. Let perseverance finish its work so that you may be mature and complete, not lacking anything." (James 1:2-4)

JULIE NELSEN

For Julie Nelsen, life has been an adventure filled with many roles as a mother of three, grandma, daughter, sister, friend, and a servant of God. She's grateful beyond words for the love experienced, and it is her heart's passion to pass that love onto others. Mission work and traveling are dreams that are currently unfolding. God has shown *unconditional love* and just as 2 Corinthians 12:9 says "His grace is sufficient enough for me, for His power is made perfect in weakness." Julie says, "I trust in the Lord to continue laying out my life, and truth be told, He is far better at it than I am."

NECKLACE SENT FROM HEAVEN

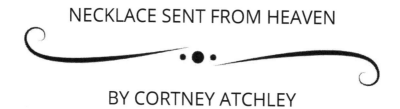

BY CORTNEY ATCHLEY

I'd like to share a miracle of how God used a broken heart, a willing person and a simple trinket, to answer a prayer and bring hope to our entire family.

I sat in the parking lot of the church, willing myself to turn off the ignition and go inside. Normally I am overjoyed to spend time rejoicing in worship, refilling my spirit with the wisdom shared with friends and refreshing my dry, thirsty bones with the living water that flowed into me, every time I walked through the doors. Today, I was struggling though. You see, very few within my church were aware of what our family had been experiencing. Living in Montana, one thousand miles away from all of my family in the Midwest, these people had become my support. The trouble was, I loved all of my church family dearly and didn't want to explain why my normally overjoyed, encouraging and spirited self was so sullen, empty, and a dried up shell, who had cried so many tears that I'd begun to feel that "empty" would now be my new normal.

Two months earlier, my family had gathered together to celebrate my younger brother's wedding, a day that my mom was desperately waiting for, so that she could attend his wedding, before her life on Earth came to an end. Following the ceremony, we got her safely back home and held a vigil by her bedside. We held hands, prayed and cried endless tears together. As she was making the transition in her final battle with Melanoma skin cancer, I truly struggled to know if my mom had fully given her heart to Christ, as I was fairly new to the "Christian" world. I knew she believed in God and angels, but I wasn't convinced she had fully accepted Jesus into her heart. She had lost her younger brother when he was sixteen, at the hands of a drunk driver and she'd never fully recovered. The deep pain from his loss, along with the trials and tribulations of life, had created a protective wall around her heart and kept her from pursuing an evident relationship with Christ. As she lay on her death bed, I asked her a few different times, "Mom, do you know Jesus?", "Mom, do you want to ask Jesus into your heart?" I would only be answered with silence. When she quietly died, my heart knew that Jesus wouldn't deny her, but my spirit wasn't truly satisfied. If she hadn't "officially" spoken the words to surrender her heart, would He accept her? I suffered quietly with the doubt, not fully confident in my mind and heart.

As I sat in the church parking lot, I felt zapped of all energy and was emotionally drained. I had spent part of my morning crying and reminiscing with my sisters, Carrie Stepp and Connie Carlson. Knowing the burdens placed on my heart, my husband and sisters encouraged me to attend a ladies' worship night. I intentionally showed up a little late, not wanting to chat with anyone, and quietly slipped into a seat in the back. As women all around me joyfully were raising their hands in worship, the heavy bricks placed upon my heart began to falter as the first, reluctant tear fell. My resolve was broken as the floodgates let loose a torrent of emotion and pain. In desperation, I quietly pled with God, "Please, Lord, I have to know if my mom is with you. I don't know how I can go on with this doubt. And if you didn't accept her, how could you accept me?" "Ask the Lord your God for a sign, whether in the deepest depths or in the highest heights." (Isaiah 7:11)

Somehow my feet began walking forward to the front where ladies were singing and praising. The hot tears flowed without shame and I knelt down at the altar, pouring all of my burdens at his feet. When the music finally ended, I felt refreshed and began gathering my things to leave, but felt a gentle tap on my shoulder. A lovely, middle aged lady was standing before me, shifting uncertainty from one foot to the other. She nervously began to speak, "I know that we haven't met before, and this is probably going to sound crazy, but tonight as we were worshipping and praying, I felt strongly that the Lord told me to give this to you." She unclasped the necklace

DREAM BOLDLY, I DARE YOU II

from around her neck and held it up to me saying "I heard that your mom died recently and felt Jesus telling me to give you this necklace. I also need to tell you that your mom is with Him. Her heart is at peace, she loves and misses you, and everything is going to be ok."

Awestruck and shaken with tears, I looked at the necklace. In her delicate hand was a simple necklace with six little square opals in the shape of a cross. Overcome by the situation, my inability to speak must have made her second guess herself, because she nervously filled the awkward silence with, "um, so, my Sister had gotten this for me on her last trip to Jerusalem where they mine opals, so this is why this necklace is so very special to me, as some people believe that Jesus was born in October rather than December. This is why the October birthstone is opal, but you don't have to take it." As she awkwardly shifted to her other foot, she began to lower her hand, as I finally snapped to my senses. I quickly wrapped her hand in mine and tearfully said, "No, you don't understand. My mom died two months ago and I have been struggling to know whether Jesus received her into heaven. Today, October 20th, is her birthday! Her birthstone is the opal, so this necklace is so special to me and through you, my prayers have been answered!" We embraced and cried together as all of the heavy doubt and pain was replaced with peace and a knowing that He is always with me. He answers all my prayers and sees all my tears.

Not only was it her birthstone, but her favorite stone of all, as Mom always wore a simple, unpretentious piece of opal jewelry. This simple, yet beautiful opal necklace sent from Heaven with love, is evidence of a treasured miracle. I hope that the sharing of my heart brings you comfort, hope and joy in knowing that God truly hears the whispers of your heart, as love endures forever.

"Do not fear, for I am with you; Do not anxiously look about you, for I am your God I will strengthen you, surely I will help you, Surely I will uphold you with My righteous right hand." (Isaiah 41:10)

CORTNEY ATCHLEY

Cortney Atchley has always embraced a spirit of adventure. She served in the Air Force as a SERE Instructor Trainee and Heavy Equipment Operator, and received her degree in Interior Design from Montana State University. Her faith is strong, and together with her husband Jesse, they instill Christ's wisdom and teachings into their five children (Colton, Christopher, Carson, Calista and Carter). She never knows what adventure God next has planned for her, but trusts she'll be equipped with knowledge, friendship, yearning and willingness to let Him lead.

WHENEVER YOU NEED ME, I WILL BE THERE

BY LAURIE THOMPSON

The following is a personal tribute in honor of a dear friend, devoted wife, loving mother, grandmother, aunt, sister, and a cherished gift to all who knew her. She was one of the most beautiful souls ever to have walked our earth. Laurie had a contagious laugh with a smile that would light up any room the moment she arrived. Laurie transitioned as a heavenly angel in December of 2016 from melanoma skin cancer. Enclosed, her family would like to share a glimpse of her heart, with the sacred messages written through her, in hopes they may inspire. Life is a gift. Remember to unwrap it fully.

With love, from Laurie:

May we wake each day with God's blessings, and sleep each night in His keeping. May we always walk in his tender care. God hears and answers. His ear is ever open to the cry of His children. Heavenly Father, thank you for the opportunity to laugh. Help me find joy in everything I do. Let me laugh and be cheerful, so that those around me will be blessed by my smile and my optimism.

I believe we all experience elements of God every day, but may not be aware. God can be seen in the details of everything that is good; like an act of kindness to a stranger, in every leaf, every wildflower, every butterfly, and every snowflake. Our earth itself is a reflection of God. God is the name given to that which we cannot understand, despite the arrogance of modern science and technology. Attempting to unravel the mystery, is a mystery. Religion is an order of organization, but faith is something we carry in our heart without an intermediate between the Lord and our self. We need God inside ourselves in order to have a conscience and values. My hope is that you'll seek an understanding of the spirit within. Our potential for spiritual growth is unlimited. For me, God is a guide, a teacher, a friend, and a protector.

Keep an open heart and an open mind. The mind when expanded by a thought, never returns to its original shape. Keep learning. Keep reflecting. Stay on the journey prepared for you. Place your life in the protection and guidance of God. See forgiveness as an action to love yourself more fully. No one has ever found serenity through hatred. Serenity is not about the ending of pain. It's about our ability to live peacefully, no matter what life brings our way. Open your eyes and look within. Are you satisfied with the life you're living? Have the courage to fail and the courage to try again.

Life can only be understood backward, yet it must be lived forward. Share the burdens of your soul with God, and seek his blessing. Leave your burdens in His hands! "Thy will be done" doesn't mean that you sit and wait. Ask to be shown the next right action. Do your part, and God will do His. Believe in yourself and all that you are. Know that there's something inside you that is greater than any obstacle.

You can start over anytime you choose, no matter what mistakes you've made. Begin again with a new attitude, a new mindset, and get on track to make things happen for you. Don't give up. Keep trying new things, as life is a work in progress. Find the best in others. Endure the betrayal of false friends. Laugh often and love much. Eat well, exercise, get lots of fresh air, meditate, recover, and spend time alone.

Prayer is a valuable mechanism for reflection, release of issues, and personal growth. Through prayer, we can heal ourself and others, relieve anxiety, solve problems and change things in our life that need changing. It is very powerful. Hope, and look forward with trust and expectant desire. Ask God for stamina to overcome and meet all the barriers that present themselves, with strength to press on when the going gets rugged.

When problems seem insurmountable, or we've lost faith

in ourselves or humanity, believe in the future. Have hope, faith and love. Love again and be loved again. Hope is a driving force in helping us stay on course in life. It may feel as though it comes and goes, but there is always hope! There's always a chance for something bright to happen. Have faith that it will. Always do what you truly believe in your heart is right, as long as you avoid hurting others in the process. As you grow stronger in your spirit and confidence, it will be harder for people to manipulate you.

Forgiveness is one of the greatest gifts of spiritual life. It enables us to be released from the sorrows of the past. Let go of resentment and outrage we have carried for too long. It washes the pain in our heart. There are many stages; grief, rage, sorrow, fear, confusion. When you feel the pain you carry, forgiveness becomes relief and a release for your heart! No matter how much pain we are in, or how self-destructive we've been, prayer is available to us; to help us find the energy we need to come back from the brink. Prayer enables us to tap into God's healing powers. Whenever I pray, things have a way of working out far better than I can imagine for myself.

If we never suffered anything, what kind of shallow, compassionless, impatient people would we be? Prayer can help maintain a positive outlook of gratitude, hope, patience and peace in the midst of suffering. Everyone goes through hard times. It's nothing to be ashamed of. Sometimes prayers help us avoid them, sometimes not. It's the attitude we have, when we go through them that matters most. God uses trials for his purpose. Whenever you feel crushed by the weight of problems, repeat: "I can do all things through Christ who strengthens me" (Philippians 4:13).

In additional to friendship, attitude is one of the few things in life where we have a true choice. We cannot change what has been fated to happen, nor the actions or events, of other people. We can change our reaction to such things with the attitude we adopt. Our attitude can be more important than anything we do. It can make or break families, companies, and nations. Attitude is more important than schooling, talent, looks or wealth. How we react is everything, and our attitude is the choice we have. It's a choice we make every minute of every day. It's a state of mind that no one can take from us. If we are in control of our attitudes, we're in command of our lives. Travel lightly. This is the best way to live.

Endings are often sad and heart-rending. There will be many throughout our life. Every day is a new beginning, a new challenge, a new chance. Ebb and flow are the cycle we are all a part of. Birth, life, growth, attachment, loss, grief, disengagement, rebirth. We must carry on, living our life the way God intended. Lord, help me be a conduit through which your healing love can flow to others.

233

Whenever you need me, I will be there:

When you're sad.

When you're happy.

When you're young.

When you're old.

When you're confused.

When you're alone.

I love you, Laurie.

If my problems have brought me to prayer, then they have served a purpose. We keep people in our hearts because it is safe there and full of love. Believe against all odds in the best of each other. You are forever in my heart. Amen.

IN LOVING MEMORY OF LAURIE THOMPSON

Laurie Thompson is a heavenly angel who always shared a contagious laugh and a smile with everyone near her. It was her wish to smile and feel joy in life every day. In her sacred writings, she shares that laughter is like a mental shampoo that washes away fears, old wounds and irritations; to promote wellness, to create a happier state of mind and to live in a state of peace. She is missed by her loving husband Jeff, her two amazing sons, Zach and Ian, and all her friends and family who loved and cherished her deeply.

THANK YOU!

We sincerely hope you've enjoyed the sharing of our hearts, the messages of hope, and our deepest desires to bring healing, peace and love to our world.

Visit DreamBoldly.org to download our Dream Boldly Challenge: 100 Dreams in 10 Days, and receive your key to unlock the eLearning course Manifest Miracles OnDemand.

Made in the USA
Lexington, KY
28 November 2017